GLOBAL ECONOMIC STUDIES

INTERNATIONAL DEBT IN INDIVIDUAL COUNTRIES

Global Economic Studies

Additional books in this series can be found on Nova's website under the Series tab.

Additional E-books in this series can be found on Nova's website under the E-books tab.

Economic Issues, Problems and Perspectives

Additional books in this series can be found on Nova's website under the Series tab.

Additional E-books in this series can be found on Nova's website under the E-books tab.

GLOBAL ECONOMIC STUDIES

INTERNATIONAL DEBT IN INDIVIDUAL COUNTRIES

ANTHONY L. MONTEFUSCO

EDITOR

Nova Science Publishers, Inc.

New York

For permission to use material from this book please contact us:
Telephone 631-231-7269; Fax 631-231-8175
Web Site: http://www.novapublishers.com

LIBRARY OF CONGRESS CATALOGING-IN-PUBLICATION DATA
International debt in individual countries / editor, Anthony L. Montefusco.
p. cm.
Includes index.
ISBN 978-1-61761-787-4 (hardcover)
1. Debts, External. 2. Debt relief. 3. Debts, Public. I. Montefusco, Anthony L.
HJ8015.I575 2011
336.3'435--dc22
2011002084

Published by Nova Science Publishers, Inc. † New York

CONTENTS

PREFACE

The global financial crisis and economic recession spurred national governments to boost fiscal expenditures to stimulate economic growth. Government measures included asset purchases, direct lending through national treasuries and government-backed guarantees for financial sector liabilities. The severity and global nature of the economic recession raised the rate of unemployment, increased the cost of stabilizing the financial sector and limited the number of policy options that were available to national leaders. This book focuses on how major developed and emerging-market country governments, particularly the G-20 and Organization for Economic Cooperation and Development (OECD) countries have dealt with the current global recession and debt crisis.

Chapter 1- The global financial crisis and economic recession spurred national governments to boost fiscal expenditures to stimulate economic growth and to provide capital injections to support their financial sectors. Government measures included asset purchases, direct lending through national treasuries, and government-backed guarantees for financial sector liabilities. The severity and global nature of the economic recession raised the rate of unemployment, increased the cost of stabilizing the financial sector, and limited the number of policy options that were available to national leaders. In turn, the financial crisis negatively affected economic output and contributed to the severity of the economic recession. As a result, the surge in fiscal spending, combined with a loss of revenue, has caused government deficit spending to rise sharply when measured as a share of gross domestic product (GDP) and increased the overall level of public debt. Recent forecasts indicate that should the current economic rebound take hold, budget deficits on the whole likely will stabilize, but are not expected to fall appreciably for some time.

Chapter 2- On May 2, 2010, the Eurozone member states and the International Monetary Fund (IMF) announced an unprecedented €110 billion (about $145 billion) financial assistance package for Greece. The following week, on May 9, 2010, EU leaders announced that they would make an additional €500 billion (about $636 billion) in financial assistance available to vulnerable European countries, and suggested that the IMF could contribute up to an additional €220 billion to €250 billion (about $280 billion to $318 billion). This chapter answers frequently asked questions about IMF involvement in the Eurozone debt crisis.

Chapter 3- Over the past decade, Greece borrowed heavily in international capital markets to fund government budget and current account deficits. The profligacy of the government, weak revenue collection, and structural rigidities in Greece's economy are typically cited as major factors behind Greece's accumulation of debt. Access to capital at low interest rates after adopting the euro and weak enforcement of EU rules concerning debt and deficit ceilings may also have played a role.

Chapter 4- In December 2001, following an extended period of economic and political instability, Argentina suffered a severe financial crisis, leading to the largest default on sovereign debt in history. It was widely recognized that Argentina faced an untenable debt situation that was in need of restructuring. In 2005, after prolonged, contentious, and unsuccessful attempts to find a mutually acceptable solution with its creditors, Argentina abandoned the negotiation process and made a one-time unilateral offer on terms highly unfavorable to the creditors. Although 76% of creditors accepted the offer, a diverse group of "holdouts" opted instead for litigation in hopes of achieving a better settlement in the future. Although Argentina succeeded in reducing much of its sovereign debt, its unorthodox methods left it ostracized from international credit markets for nearly a decade and triggered legislative action and sanctions in the United States.

Chapter 5- After several years of surpluses in the late 1990s, the federal budget has been in deficit since FY2001. Deficits represent the additional borrowing required in each year to bridge the gap between tax revenues and spending outlays. Each deficit adds to the already existing stock of outstanding federal debt.

Some of those deficits may have seemed large at the time, but the budget deficit for FY2009 was unprecedented, in dollar terms, and the FY2010 deficit is also expected to be much larger than those of past years. The prospect of such rapid growth in the federal debt may seem alarming, and some might wonder how much the debt can grow before it poses significant economic risks.

Chapter 6- Following the ouster of the Saddam Hussein regime in spring 2003, Iraq's external debt was estimated to be around $130 billion. Reducing this debt to a sustainable level has been a priority of the U.S. government. Since 2003, debt relief negotiations have taken place in a variety of fora and led to the cancellation of a significant amount of Iraq's external debt.

In: International Debt in Individual Countries ISBN: 978-1-61761-787-4
Editors: Anthony L. Montefusco

Chapter 1

LIMITING CENTRAL GOVERNMENT BUDGET DEFICITS: INTERNATIONAL EXPERIENCES

James K. Jackson

SUMMARY

The global financial crisis and economic recession spurred national governments to boost fiscal expenditures to stimulate economic growth and to provide capital injections to support their financial sectors. Government measures included asset purchases, direct lending through national treasuries, and government-backed guarantees for financial sector liabilities. The severity and global nature of the economic recession raised the rate of unemployment, increased the cost of stabilizing the financial sector, and limited the number of policy options that were available to national leaders. In turn, the financial crisis negatively affected economic output and contributed to the severity of the economic recession. As a result, the surge in fiscal spending, combined with a loss of revenue, has caused government deficit spending to rise sharply when measured as a share of gross domestic product (GDP) and increased the overall level of public debt. Recent forecasts indicate that should the current economic rebound take hold, budget deficits on the whole likely will stabilize, but are not expected to fall appreciably for some time.

The sharp rise in deficit spending is prompting policymakers to assess various strategies for winding down their stimulus measures and to curtail capital injections without disrupting the nascent economic recovery. This chapter focuses on how major developed and emerging-market country governments, particularly the G-20 and Organization for Economic Cooperation and Development (OECD) countries, limit their fiscal deficits. Financial markets support government efforts to reduce deficit spending, because they are concerned over the long-term impact of the budget deficits. At the same time, they are concerned that the loss of spending will slow down the economic recovery and they doubt the conviction of some governments to impose austere budgets in the face of public opposition. Some central governments are examining such measures as budget rules, or fiscal consolidation, as a way to trim spending and reduce the overall size of their central government debt. Budget rules can be applied in a number of ways, including limiting central government budget deficits to a determined percentage of GDP. To the extent that fiscal consolidation lowers the market rate of interest, such efforts could improve a government's budget position by lowering borrowing costs and stimulating economic growth. Other strategies include authorizing independent public institutions to spearhead fiscal consolidation efforts and developing medium-term budgetary frameworks for fiscal planning. Fiscal consolidation efforts, however, generally require policymakers to weigh the effects of various policy trade-offs, including the trade-off between adopting stringent, but enforceable, rules-based programs, compared with more flexible, but less effective, principles-based programs that offer policymakers some discretion in applying punitive measures.

Overview and Background

In its recent economic outlook,[1] the International Monetary Fund (IMF) indicated that fiscal balances, or the annual budget balance, of the economically advanced G-20[2] countries weakened by 6 percentage points of GDP between 2007 and 2009, rising from 1.9% to 7.9% of GDP. The largest impact on the fiscal balances of the advanced G-20 countries was projected to occur in 2009 and 2010. Also, the forecast indicates that government debt, or the accumulated amount of government deficits, among the advanced G-20 countries will rise on average by 14.5% of GDP by the end of 2009, compared with 2007, as indicated in **Table 1**.[3] This forecast is considered by the IMF to represent the middle of the range of estimates, and it is based on the assumption that the economic recovery will continue at the pace experienced in mid-2009. In the same forecast, the annual budget deficits for the emerging

G-20 countries were projected to widen on average from a surplus of 0.2% of GDP in 2007 to a deficit of 3.2% of GDP in 2009, while government debt was expected to remain at a constant share of GDP. For European governments, the rise in government budget deficits and the increase in the total amount of government debt is undermining their efforts to reduce the size of their annual central government budget deficits. These estimates for the growth in government debt could change, depending on the success governments have in liquidating at favorable prices the assets they acquired during the financial crisis, the timing and strength of the economic recovery, and the extent of any payout on official guarantees.

The magnitude and pervasive nature of the government deficits is unsettling international capital markets. In general, public sector debts are rising relative to national gross domestic product (GDP), the broadest measure of a nation's economic output. The international markets also have become increasingly wary of rising government deficits due to an increased perception of risk. In particular, these perceived risks are viewed as being especially high in Europe where financial institutions are exposed to economic troubles in Greece, Portugal, and Spain. According to the Bank for International Settlements (BIS) the euro area banks hold more than 70% of the outstanding public sector debt of Greece.[4] Furthermore, the uneven pace of the economic recovery is adding to perceptions of risk.

Generally, the rising level of public sector debts in most countries do not reflect profligate spending, but reflect measures policymakers adopted to avert a more serious and protracted economic recession. Nevertheless, policymakers and financial markets are especially concerned over the situation in Europe, where some investors view the rising deficits in Portugal, Spain, Greece, and Ireland as increasing the risks for a default and the potential for additional turmoil in the financial markets.[5] In some cases, these countries have borrowed heavily from the European Central Bank (ECB). The ECB requires borrower countries to provide government bonds rated above BBB- as collateral, but that minimum rating is expected to rise to A- by the end of the 2010 and would rule out Greek bonds if rating agencies continue to downgrade the sovereign bonds.

For this and other reasons, the economic conditions of Portugal, Greece, Spain, and Ireland were a key topic at the early February 2010 meeting of G7 finance ministers and the exchange value of the euro has depreciated against the dollar recently amid broader concerns over the impact budget deficits will have on the larger economies in the Eurozone.[6] Such concerns could tighten credit and raise borrowing costs for a broad number of countries. Rather than relying on the International Monetary Fund to provide loans to the four countries in the most immediate danger, the richer economies of the Eurozone, particularly France and Germany, may well step in and provide loans and other assistance to those nations in trouble. Prospects of a default by any member of the Eurozone, however, could severely strain the cohesion of the zone and challenge some aspects of European economic integration.

In addition to the IMF's projections, the latest Economic Outlook[7] by the Organization for Economic Cooperation and Development (OECD) also projects an economic recovery to begin in 2010. The OECD estimates, however, that economic performance among OECD countries on average after 2010 will be below that experienced in the period prior to the financial crisis. According to the OECD, most developed countries will continue to face severe imbalances within their economies, including low levels of output, low levels of private investment, high rates of unemployment (including a higher rate of permanent unemployment), low inflation, and large central government deficits. As OECD economists have noted,[8] economic downturns that follow a banking crisis typically last longer and involve greater losses in economic output and a greater deterioration in the fiscal balances of central governments than economic recessions not associated with a banking crisis. In most of the cases studied by OECD economists, the banking crises usually involved a single country or a small group of countries. As a result, those countries were able to export their way out of their economic recession. In the current environment, however, one could argue that few of the large number of countries that are concurrently experiencing an economic recession likely will succeed in exporting their way to an economic recovery.

Impact on Central Government Budgets

The current financial and economic crises have worsened the financial position of the central government budgets of the G-20 countries, although the impact of the crises has varied by country. The two crises are affecting the balance sheets of the central governments in three broad areas. First, governments adopted a broad range of special measures to support the financial system. Second, policymakers adopted discretionary fiscal stimulus measures to spur economic growth in order to stem the effects of the sharp drop in economic activity. Third, most economies experienced a loss in tax revenue and a surge in non-discretionary spending, referred to as automatic stabilizers, including such activities as unemployment insurance, that rise without direct legislative authorization. As a result of these factors, the financial crisis has undermined the effectiveness of budget rules as government budgets are affected by large or prolonged internal or external shocks.

Table 2 displays the combination of these three spending activities on the overall balance of G-20 countries. The data indicate that over the 2009-2010 period, the overall fiscal balance for the United States is expected to fall from -5.9% to -8.9% of GDP as automatic stabilizers kick in and as discretionary policy actions, in the form of deficit spending, increase. Additionally, the data indicate that the U.S. budget balance is being affected almost equally by automatic stabilizers, discretionary fiscal policy actions, and by other actions, including extraordinary measures, that were taken to shore up the financial sector. In comparison, Saudi Arabia and Russia experienced a double-digit deterioration in their budget balances as their government budgets shifted from running a surplus to being in deficit, due in large part to the drop in oil revenues as the price of oil fell during the economic recession. Saudi Arabia also adopted other discretionary fiscal measures that contributed to its budget deficit. Great Britain, as is the case with other G-20 members, adopted discretionary spending measures. Those measures, however, were less a factor in driving up its budget deficits than spending associated with automatic stabilizers.

The OECD also has estimated the impact of spending increases and the loss of tax revenue on the budget balances of major economies that are associated with the fiscal stimulus packages that the developed economies adopted, as indicated in **Table 3**. On average, a decrease in tax revenue and an increase in spending due to the stimulus packages adopted by the developed countries in 2008 to counter the economic recession and the financial crisis are expected to have a relatively equal impact on the budget balances of the developed countries. For the United States, the loss in tax revenue is expected to have a larger negative impact on the budget balance than the negative effect associated with a higher level of spending. The OECD estimates indicate that the economic recovery that began in 2009 will stem the continued deterioration in budget balances in 2010, but that it likely will not be a strong enough recovery to turn around the budget balances in most of the larger economies.

Table 1. Fiscal Balance and Government Debt of G-20 Countries (expressed as a percent of national GDP)

	Fiscal Balance					Government Gross Debt				
Country	2007	2008	2009	2010	2014	2007	2008	2009	2010	2014
Argentina	-2.3%	-0.5%	-3.6%	-2.3%	-0.4%	65.9%	49.2%	38.6%	33.7%	23.5%
Australia	1.6	1.7	1.8	1.7	1.7	8.9	8.1	7.9	7.2	4.2
Brazil	-2.2	-1.1	-1.3	-1.2	-0.6	67.7	65.4	64.7	62.9	54.1
Canada	1.4	0.5	-1.5	-1.9	2.1	64.2	60.8	63.0	62.6	46.5
China	0.9	-0.1	-2.0	-2.0	-0.5	20.2	17.9	22.2	23.4	18.6
France	-2.7	-3.3	-5.5	-6.3	-2.7	63.9	66.1	72.3	77.1	79.4
Germany	-0.2	-0.1	-3.3	-4.6	0.1	65.0	68.7	76.1	80.1	77.2
India	-5.2	-7.8	-8.5	-7.4	-4.5	80.5	80.6	82.7	82.9	71.6
Indonesia	-1.2	0.1	-2.6	-2.0	-1.6	35.0	32.5	31.8	31.3	28.3
Italy	-1.6	-2.7	-3.9	-4.3	-4.2	104.1	105.6	109.4	112.4	118.0
Japan	-3.4	-4.7	-7.1	-7.2	-6.4	195.5	202.5	217.0	225.1	222.3
Korea	3.8	1.4	-0.8	-0.8	0.6	32.1	32.8	32.9	33.0	29.3
Mexico	-1.4	-1.7	-2.9	-2.8	-2.3	38.3	39.3	42.1	42.5	42.0
Russia	6.8	5.3	-2.6	-2.0	-3.5	7.3	5.8	6.5	6.5	6.4
Saudi Arabia	15.8	35.0	-1.2	1.7	2.6	18.7	12.9	11.6	9.7	5.8
South Africa	0.9	-0.2	-1.9	-1.7	-0.3	28.5	27.2	27.0	26.7	22.2
Spain	2.2	-3.1	-6.1	-6.0	-2.1	36.2	38.6	48.6	53.8	56.3
Turkey	-2.3	-2.5	-2.3	-2.0	0.3	38.9	38.7	40.4	40.4	29.7
United Kingdom	-2.7	-4.2	-7.2	-8.1	-4.8	44.0	50.4	61.0	68.7	76.2
United States	-2.9	-6.4	-12.0	-8.9	-5.1	63.1	68.7	81.2	90.2	99.5

Table 1. (Continued)

	Fiscal Balance					Government Gross Debt				
Country	**2007**	**2008**	**2009**	**2010**	**2014**	**2007**	**2008**	**2009**	**2010**	**2014**
G-20	-1.1	-2.6	-6.2	-5.3	-3.0	63.5	65.5	72.5	76.7	76.8
Advanced G-20 Countries	-1.9	-4.1	-7.9	-6.8	-3.8	78.8	83.2	93.2	99.8	103.5
Emerging Market G-20 Countries	0.2	-0.1	-3.2	-2.8	NA	37.7	35.7	37.6	37.8	32.0

Source: *The State of Pubic Finances: Outlook and Medium-Term Policies After the 2008 Crash*, the International Monetary Fund, March 6, 2009, Table 6.

Table 2. Overall Central Government Budget Balances, Automatic Stabilizers and Discretionary Measures of G-20 Countries (as a percent of GDP)

	Overall Balance				Average Annual Change in 2008-2010 compared to 2007			
	2007	**2008**	**2009**	**2010**	**Overall Balance**	**Automatic Stabilizers**	**Discretionary Measures**	**Other**
Argentina	-2.3	-0.5	-3.6	-2.3	0.2	-0.6	-0.4	1.2
Australia	1.6	0.1	-2.2	-2.8	-3.3	-1.7	-1.5	0.0
Brazil	-2.2	-1.5	-1.0	-0.8	1.1	-0.7	-0.2	2.0
Canada	1.4	0.4	-3.2	-3.7	-3.6	-1.8	-0.9	-0.9
China	0.9	-0.3	-3.6	-3.6	-3.4	-0.6	-2.1	-0.7
France	-2.7	-3.1	-6.0	-6.2	-2.5	-2.4	-0.4	0.3
Germany	-0.2	-0.1	-4.0	-5.2	-3.0	-1.6	-1.1	-0.2
India	-5.2	-8.4	-10	-8.6	-3.8	-0.4	-0.4	-3.0
Indonesia	-1.2	0.1	-2.5	-2.1	-0.3	-0.1	-0.6	0.5

Table 2. (Continued)

	Overall Balance				Average Annual Change in 2008-2010 compared to 2007			
	2007	2008	2009	2010	Overall Balance	Automatic Stabilizers	Discretionary Measures	Other
Italy	-1.5	-2.7	-4.8	-5.2	-2.7	-2.6	-0.1	0.0
Japan	-3.4	-5.0	-8.1	-8.3	-3.7	-2.2	-0.7	-0.9
Korea	3.8	1.2	-2.2	-3.2	-5.1	-1.5	-1.6	-2.1
Mexico	-1.4	-1.9	-3.2	-2.9	-1.3	-1.3	-0.5	0.6
Russia	6.8	4.2	-5.2	-5.1	-8.8	-1.4	-1.3	-6.1
Saudi Arabia	15.8	35.5	-8.3	-6.5	-8.9	-0.5	-3.1	-5.4
South Africa	0.9	-0.1	-2.7	-3.4	-3.0	-0.6	-1.0	-1.5
Turkey	-2.1	-3.0	-4.2	-3.3	-1.4	-2.1	0.0	0.7
United Kingdom	-2.7	-5.5	-9.5	-11.0	-6.0	-2.5	-0.5	-2.9
United States	-2.9	-5.9	-7.7	-8.9	-4.6	-1.6	-1.6	-1.4
G-20 PPP GDP- Weighted average	-1.1	-2.6	-5.9	-6.3	-3.8	-1.4	-1.2	-1.2
Memorandum item: EU G-20	-1.6	-2.7	-6.0	-6.9	-3.5	-2.2	-0.6	-0.7

Source: *Global Economic* Policies and Prospects, IMF Staff Note for the Group of Twenty Meeting, March 13-14, 2009, the International Monetary Fund.

Notes: PPP stands for purchasing power parity, or the data have been adjusted to account for exchange rates. The three spending areas are: 1) automatic stabilizers, or those governments payments that are ratcheted up automatically as the rate of economic growth slows (unemployment insurance, for instance); 2) discretionary measures, or macroeconomic policy actions that were taken specifically to address the economic downturn; 3) other expenditures, such as fiscal expenditures to shore up distressed banks; and 4) the overall balance, or the combination of the three effects. Negative numbers indicate deficit spending as a percent of GDP.

Table 3. Size and Timing of Fiscal Packages (Change in central government budget balances by component and period)

	2008-2010 net effect on fiscal balance			Distribution over the period		
	Spending	Tax revenue	Total	2008	2009	2010
	Percent of 2008 GDP			Percent of total net effect		
Australia	-4.1%	-1.3%	-5.4%	13.0%	54.0%	33.0%
Austria	-0.4	-0.8	-1.2	0.0	79.0	21.0
Belgium	-1.1	-0.3	-1.4	0.0	51.0	49.0
Canada	-1.7	-2.4	-4.1	12.0	41.0	47.0
Czech Republic	-0.3	-2.5	-2.8	0.0	56.0	44.0
Denmark	-2.6	-0.7	-3.3	0.0	33.0	67.0
Finland	-0.5	-2.7	-3.2	0.0	47.0	53.0
France	-0.6	-0.2	-0.7	0.0	68.0	32.0
Germany	-1.6	-1.6	-3.2	0.0	48.0	52.0
Greece	0.0	0.8	0.8	0.0	100.0	NA
Hungary	7.5	0.2	7.7	0.0	51.0	49.0
Iceland	1.6	5.7	7.3	0.0	28.0	72.0
Ireland	2.2	6.0	8.3	6.0	39.0	55.0
Italy	-0.3	0.3	0	0.0	15.0	85.0
Japan	-4.2	-0.5	-4.7	2.0	74.0	25.0
Korea	-3.2	-2.8	-6.1	17.0	62.0	21.0
Luxembourg	-1.6	-2.3	-3.9	0.0	65.0	35.0

Table 3. (Continued)

	2008-2010 net effect on fiscal balance			Distribution over the period		
	Spending	Tax revenue	Total	2008	2009	2010
	Percent of 2008 GDP			Percent of total net effect		
Mexico	-1.2	-0.4	-1.6	0.0	100.0	NA
Netherlands	-0.9	-1.6	-2.5	0.0	49.0	51.0
New Zealand	0.3	-4.1	-3.7	6.0	54.0	40.0
Norway	-0.9	-0.3	-1.2	0.0	100.0	NA
Poland	-0.8	-0.4	-1.2	0.0	70.0	30.0
Portugal	..	..	-0.8	0.0	100.0	0.0
Slovak Republic	-0.7	-0.7	-1.3	0.0	41.0	59.0
Spain	-2.2	-1.7	-3.9	32.0	44.0	23.0
Sweden	-1.7	-1.7	-3.3	0.0	43.0	57.0
Switzerland	-0.3	-0.2	-0.5	0.0	68.0	32.0
Turkey	-2.9	-1.5	-4.4	17.0	46.0	37.0
United Kingdom	-0.4	-1.5	-1.9	11.0	85.0	4.0
United States	-2.4	-3.2	-5.6	21.0	37.0	42.0
Major seven	-2.1	-2	-4.1	15.0	47.0	38.0
OECD average	-0.9	-0.9	-1.7	12.0	60.0	28.0

Source: Official Packages Across OECD Countries: Overview and Country Details, Organization for Economic Cooperation and Development, March 31, 2009.

This continued erosion in budget balances through 2010 is raising concerns among some policymakers who contend that the budget deficits will undermine market confidence in their governments. As a result of these concerns, some analysts argue that capital markets will grow reluctant to finance the budget deficits without greater compensation in the form of higher returns, which would add to the overall cost of the deficits. In a recent report, however, the IMF concluded that a rise in the level of the central government's debt, by itself, does not necessarily have a major adverse impact on a government's solvency and, therefore, on financial markets. Nevertheless, the IMF cautions that the rise in government debt represents an important challenge that should not be ignored. The IMF contends that the source of the rise in government debt is a factor in market confidence. According to the IMF, the current rise in government deficits for most countries does not represent an explosive upward path in spending, but represents targeted and necessary policy responses to the financial and economic crises. A rise in government debt that is directed at stemming an economic recession or a financial crisis does not necessarily undermine market confidence as long as governments can undertake credible programs to reduce spending once the crisis has been averted. With some notable exceptions such as Greece, the rise in spending generally is not viewed as representing profligate spending by central governments, but is attributed to measures to address the financial crisis, including spending on social programs that rise without overt discretionary actions. Such automatic stabilizers have an especially large impact on the spending of governments within the European Union, where the government sector accounts for a larger share of total GDP.

FISCAL CONSOLIDATION: COUNTRY EFFORTS

Since 1990, numerous national governments in developed countries have undertaken fiscal consolidation efforts, often by adopting a budgetary rule that restricts the size of the annual amount of the government budget deficit to a certain percentage of GDP. The reasons for fiscal consolidations are as varied as the governments themselves. Most often, policymakers are motivated to reduce the government's budget deficit due to a variety of concerns. These include: the rising pressure on public finances of aging populations; the cost of financing a rising amount of debt; the impact on price inflation; the crowding out of private investment; and the reputation and credibility of the government and its economic policies in the financial markets. **Table 4** details fourteen instances between 1990 and 2005 identified by the IMF in which governments in developed countries undertook fiscal consolidation. As is indicated, these efforts generally were initiated for a short period of time and were designed to meet a specific objective. The details provided by the IMF include the political and macroeconomic environment in which the fiscal consolidation occurred and the condition of the central governments' budget. In a number of cases, budget consolidation can be associated with a change in governments in which the budget deficit was an issue in the preceding election.

The IMF concluded that successful fiscal consolidation efforts generally were accompanied by a supportive domestic and international environment, including, but not limited to, periods of sustained positive economic growth among trading partners. While fiscal consolidation generally tends to reduce the overall rate of growth in an economy in the short run due to the drop in the central government's contribution to GDP growth, the IMF authors concluded that: 1) this negative effect was not as pronounced as had been indicated in previous studies; 2) that in some cases fiscal consolidation had a positive impact on the rate of economic growth; and 3) that the long-term impact on economic growth from a reduction in central government spending depended on a range of factors, including the strength of private domestic demand.[9]

To reduce the size of the government's deficit spending, policymakers have a number of options. These options include reducing current spending, increasing current revenue, reducing capital spending, or some combination of spending reductions and revenue increases. While the record on the economic effects of these various approaches to fiscal consolidation is mixed, a study by the OECD concluded that "spending restraint (notably with respect to government consumption and transfers) is more likely to generate lasting fiscal consolidation and better economic performance" than revenue enhancements.[10] Despite this general result, the OECD study also concluded that the experiences of OECD countries was that revenue increases "accounted for a larger fraction of the total reduction,"[11] than did reductions in government spending. In addition, the study concluded that three-fourths of the episodes involved a combination of cuts in government expenditures and increases in government revenues. Reductions in capital spending generally played a small role in such fiscal consolidation efforts, according to the OECD study.

Table 4. Fiscal Consolidation Efforts in Selected Developed Countries

Episode	Political Background	Macroeconomic Background	Government Finances
Canada, 1994–97	Majority federal government elected in 1993 to address fiscal issues; similar election result in 1994-95 in the two largest provinces.	Recovery from recession; low inflation; high output gap and unemployment; exchange rate deprecation; improving current account balance.	Sizable deficit and debt stock; large share of debt held at short term and by non-residents; high tax-to-GDP ratio; expending entitlements; sub-federal fiscal issues.
Denmark, 2004–05	The ruling center-right coalition entered the second half of its term with a diminishing voter support.	Continued economic slowdown (since 2001) characterized by gradually rising unemployment.	A moderate level of public debt (of about 50% of GDP), a near- balanced budget.
Finland, 1998	Both the coalition elected in 1991 and the grand coalition elected in 1995 had a clear mandate for EMU membership.	Gradual consolidation (from 1992) started at the time of deep recession characterized by high output gap, rising unemployment, low inflation, and depreciating exchange rate. By 1998 the economy had recovered and enjoyed a growth rate well above the EU average.	High deficit and medium-level but rapidly increasing debt, high tax-to-GDP ratio and expanding entitlement programs.
France, 1996–97	The president brought forward parliamentary elections by one year to ensure that the new government had a clear mandate for fiscal	The consolidation was launched against the background of a slow recovery from a recession, characterized by relatively high unemployment, low inflation, and exchange rate depreciation.	The expansionary policy in response to the 1993 recession left France with a large fiscal deficit and a medium-level but rapidly rising public debt, falling

Table 4. (Continued)

Episode	Political Background	Macroeconomic Background	Government Finances
	consolidation and that domestic elections did not interfere with the pre-EMU meeting of the European Council in early 1998.		short of the EMU criteria.
Germany, 2003–05	The coalition led by the Social-Democratic Party narrowly won the elections in September 2002. The comprehensive reform plan (Agenda 2010) was unveiled in March 2003.	Three years of static output, high unemployment, concerns about possible deflation, heavy losses in the financial sector.	Fiscal deficit widened to about 3.7% of GDP in 2002, with public debt hovering around 60% of GDP.
Ireland, 2003–04	The coalition government enjoyed a strong parliamentary majority since 2002. In addition, there were few differences of views within the coalition.	After a decade of strong growth, economic activity (excluding profits of multinationals) decelerated markedly in 2002 and remained subdued in 2003.	Relatively low level of public debt (below 35% of GDP), a near-balanced budget, a relatively low tax-to-GDP ratio.
Italy, 1997	The consolidation was preceded by the electoral reforms at both the central and regional levels, which resulted in more stable governments with longer	The consolidation attempt was launched during the time when growth turned negative in late 1996 - early 1997 after strong performance in 1995, and the return of the recession of the early 1990s was perceived as likely. Inflation was	Very high debt (of over 115% of GDP in 1997), rising in spite of fiscal consolidation attempts since early 1990s.

Table 4. (Continued)

Episode	Political Background	Macroeconomic Background	Government Finances
	political horizons.	declining but the unemployment remained high.	
Japan, 2004	Ruling coalition since 2000. In 2004, the positions of the ruling party in both houses of parliament shrank as the government's approval rating hit the low of 36 percent (compared to 70–90% in 2001), partly due to the passage of pension reforms.	Gradual economic recovery since mid-2002, with contributions from both exports and domestic demand, characterized by gradually declining unemployment and easing of deflation.	A decade of high fiscal deficits (about 8 percent of GDP in 2003) led to a rapid accumulation of public debt, which reached 160% of GDP. The revenue-to-GDP ratio remained below 30%, while social security outlays kept rising.
Netherlands, 2004–05	As a result of early elections in January 2003, center-right coalition government took office.	There had been a significant downturn in activity since 2000. During the two years, growth averaged barely 0.2%, with unemployment rising. Activity began to pick up in 2004 and growth was projected at about 1% in 2004 and 1¾% in 2005. The authorities had the challenge of nurturing the emerging recovery while ensuring fiscal	There had been a sharp deterioration in the fiscal position with the 3 percent Maastricht deficit ceiling breached in 2003. The general government balance worsened by almost 5½ percentage points during the first three years of the decade, as a result of the 2001 tax reform, increases in health care and education spending,

Table 4. (Continued)

Episode	Political Background	Macroeconomic Background	Government Finances
		sustainability.	and a higher deficit of local governments (reaching 0.6 percent of GDP).
New Zealand, 2003	Competitive political environment, with the opposition calling on the ruling Labor Party to introduce more tax cuts and improve the quality of health and education services. However, the September 2005 elections did not lead to any significant relaxation of fiscal policy and the incumbent party was re-elected with a confirmed mandate for continued fiscal consolidation.	Solid and accelerating economic growth, narrowing current account deficit, unemployment at a 16-year low.	A slight budget surplus and a moderate level of public debt (of about 40% of GDP), which exceeded, however, the government's long-term target of 30% of GDP.
Spain, 1996–97	Elected in March 1996, the coalition government had a mandate for fiscal consolidation.	A relatively rapid economic recovery after the recession that culminated in a negative growth in 1993. While economic activity was on the rise and inflation gradually subsided, high unemployment (at above 20% of labor	Public finances have gradually deteriorated since 1988 with annual fiscal deficits exceeding 7% of GDP in 1995. Public debt has rapidly risen to over 70%

Table 4. (Continued)

Episode	Political Background	Macroeconomic Background	Government Finances
		force) proved to be persistent.	of GDP.
Sweden, 1994–98	The Social Democrat minority government launched fiscal consolidation following the 1994 general elections.	The deepest recession since the 1930s, accompanied by high inflation, quickly rising unemployment, exchange rate depreciation and associated improvement in the current account balance.	Fiscal deficit exploded to over 12% of GDP as a result of the cyclical downturn and the underfinanced tax reform of 1990–91, with public debt reaching 80% of GDP.
United Kingdom, 1995–98	The popularity of the Conservative party by the middle of the term was low. After 18 years of being in opposition, the Labor Party won elections in May 1997 with an overwhelming majority in Parliament. The new government confirmed the course of fiscal Consolidation and introduced a number of new policy reforms, including transferring the responsibility for setting interest rates from the Treasury to the Bank of England.	Three successive years of solid economic growth, led by private consumption. Unemployment was falling rapidly, while inflation remained relatively low.	Public sector fiscal deficit increased to over 7 percent of GDP by 1994, the debt-to-GDP ratio was on the rise and already exceeded the target level of 40% by about 8 percentage points.

Table 4. (Continued)

Episode	Political Background	Macroeconomic Background	Government Finances
United States, 1994	New Democratic President took over in January 1993. The Congress was also Democratic and there was expectation of an initiative to reduce debt.	Economic activity had been weak for some time, and unemployment was rising.	The federal government fiscal situation had been deteriorating at a sharp pace. The deficit was almost 5% of GDP. In nominal terms federal debt had quadrupled over 1980–92 and the debt ratio was projected to continue rising at a high rate.

Source: Kumar, Manmohan S., Daniel Leigh, and Alexander Plekhanov, *Fiscal Adjustments: Determinants and Macroeconomic Consequences,* International Monetary Fund, IMF Working Paper WP/07/1 78, July 1007, p. 10-11.

BUDGET RULES

One approach developed countries have used to address government budget deficits has been to adopt some type of a budget rule. A study by the OECD on fiscal consolidation concluded that most developed countries have at some time adopted budget rules that restrict the amount of deficit spending to a specified percent of GDP and that constrain the overall level of the central government's debt, as indicated in **Table 5.**[12] One common feature of these rules is that most of them were applied for a relatively short period of time. In contrast, members of the European Union (EU), which account for half of the total number of developed countries, have adopted both short-term, country-specific budget rules, and long-term EU-wide budget rules.

Table 5. Fiscal Rules Being Applied in Developed Countries

		Characteristics of the set of rules			
Country	**Name and date**	**Budget target**	**Expenditure target**	**Rule to deal with windfall revenues**	**Golden rule**
Australia	Charter of Budget Honesty (1998)	yes	no	no	no
Austria	Stability and Growth Pact (1997) Domestic Stability Pact (2000)	yes	no	no	no
Belgium	Stability and Growth Pact (1997) National budget rule (2000)	yes	no	yes	no
Canada	Debt repayment plan (1998)	yes	no	yes	no
Czech republic	Stability and Growth Pact (2004) Law on budgetary rules (2004)	yes	yes	no	no
Denmark	Medium term fiscal strategy (1998)	yes	yes	no	no
Finland	Stability and Growth Pact (1997)	yes	yes	no	no

Table 5. (Continued)

		Characteristics of the set of rules			
Country	**Name and date**	**Budget target**	**Expenditure target**	**Rule to deal with windfall revenues**	**Golden rule**
	Spending limits (1991, revised in 1995 and 1998)				
France	Stability and Growth Pact (1997) Central Government Expenditure Ceiling (1998)	yes	yes	Since 2006	no
Germany	Stability and Growth Pact (1997) Domestic Stability Pact (2002)	yes	yes	no	yes
Greece	Stability and Growth Pact (1997)	yes	no	no	no
Hungary	Stability and Growth Pact (2004)	yes	no	no	no
Ireland	Stability and Growth Pact (1997)	yes	no	no	no
Italy	Stability and Growth Pact (1997) Nominal ceiling on expenditure growth (2002)	yes	yes	no	no
Japan	Cabinet decision on the Medium Term Fiscal Perspective (2002)	yes	yes	no	no
Luxem-bourg	Stability and Growth Pact (1997) Coalition agreement on expenditure ceiling (1999, 2004)	yes	no	no	no
Mexico	Budget and Fiscal Responsibility Law (2006)	yes	no	yes	no
Nether-lands	Stability and Growth Pact (1997)	yes	yes	yes	no

Table 5. (Continued)

		Characteristics of the set of rules			
Country	**Name and date**	**Budget target**	**Expenditure target**	**Rule to deal with windfall revenues**	**Golden rule**
	Coalition agreement on multiyear expenditure targets (1994, revised in 2003)				
New Zealand	Fiscal Responsibility Act (1994)	yes	yes	no	no
Norway	Fiscal Stability Guidelines (2001)	yes	no	yes	no
Poland	Stability and Growth Pact (2004) Act on Public Finance (1999)	yes	no	no	no
Portugal	Stability and Growth Pact (1997)	yes	no	no	no
Slovak Republic	Stability and Growth Pact (2004)	yes	no	no	no
Spain	Stability and Growth Pact (1997) Fiscal Stability Law (2004)	yes	no	no	no
Sweden	Fiscal Budget Act (1996, revised in 1999)	yes	yes	no	no
Switzer-land	Debt containment rule (2001, but in force since 2003)	yes	yes	yes	no
United Kingdom	Code for Fiscal Stability (1998)	yes	no	no	yes

Source: Guichard, Stephanie, Mike Kennedy, Eckhard Wurzel, and Christophe Andre, *What Promotes Fiscal Consolidation: OECD Country Experiences*, Organization for Economic Cooperation and Development [EC/WKP(2007) 13], 2007.

Notes: The Golden Rule generally restricts central governments from borrowing to fund current spending. Borrowing to fund investments generally is exempted from the budget rules. Essentially, the rule attempts to equate current spending with current revenues.

In general, the OECD concluded after observing fiscal consolidation efforts among OECD countries since 1990 that the more successful of these efforts combined rules to balance the budget with requirements to reduce expenditures. The study argues that no one rule fits all countries and all circumstances, but that successful programs of consolidation seem to have some common features. These features include rules that are simple to manage, while incorporating enough flexibility, or discretion, to respond to downturns in the business cycles. The OECD study also observed that budget rules that rely on reducing expenditures generally have been more successful. By focusing on expenditures, the rules were more successful because: 1) they were not reliant on cyclically volatile revenues; 2) they were designed to let economic stabilizers work during a downturn; and 3) they saved windfall gains during an upturn. The data in **Table 5** also indicate if the budget rules include provisions for dealing with windfall surpluses and a "Golden Rule" provision. A golden rule provision requires that the central government's current expenditures match its current revenues, exclusive of capital investments.

BUDGET RULES IN EUROPE: THE STABILITY AND GROWTH PACT

In contrast to the short-term, country-specific budget rules most OECD countries have adopted at various times to address rising central government budget deficits, the members of the EU also operate within the requirements of the Stability and Growth Pact, which was adopted in 1997. EU members decided that, due to the disparate performance and composition of their economies, it was necessary to adopt a fiscal rule in lieu of relying on market forces to coordinate their economic policies. The Pact consists of preventive measures that include monitoring the fiscal policies of the members by the European Commission and the European Council so that fiscal discipline is maintained and enforced in the Economic and Monetary Union (EMU). The Pact also includes corrective measures that provide for fines for countries that fail over a number of years to meet the Pact's requirements. The European Union comprises the largest single bloc of countries that collectively have applied a long-term set of rules. These rules require the members to apply corrective measures to reduce their annual budget deficits and to reduce the overall level of their government debt if the annual deficits or the overall amount of debt exceed certain prescribed percentages of GDP. Since the Stability and Growth Pact was adopted, however, it has not always been applied consistently, which eventually led the EU to amend the Pact.

The basic elements of the Stability and Growth Pact did not originate with the Pact itself, but were part of the original Maastricht Treaty that served as the founding document for the present- day EU. The budget rules are based on Articles 99 and 104 of the Treaty, and related decisions, including the excessive deficit procedure protocol. Article 99 of the Treaty requires the members to "regard their economic policies as a matter of common concern." They also are required to coordinate their economic policies in order to have "similar economic performance." Article 104 requires EU members to "avoid excessive government deficits." EU members are expected to follow established guidelines regarding the ratio of the government deficit relative to GDP and the ratio of government debt to gross domestic product. The Protocol on Excessive Deficit Procedure established the specific guidelines that are applied under Article 104. Under this protocol, EU members are expected to have an annual budget deficit no greater than 3% of GDP at market prices and government debt no more than an amount equivalent to 60% of GDP. The number of member states with a fiscal deficit above 3% of GDP increased from two in 2007 to twenty in 2010.[13]

All of the members of the EU are expected to meet the requirement of the budget rules. Nevertheless, the rules are of especial importance to the group of countries known as the euro area, because the members have adopted the euro as their common currency. Typically, countries have a set of economic policy tools available to them to manage their economies. These macroeconomic policy tools generally include such monetary and fiscal policy measures as control over the nation's money supply, adjustments in tax rates, and control over government spending. In addition, nations have tools to affect the international exchange value of their currency. By adopting a common currency, however, the euro area countries ceded control of their currency to the European Central Bank. Consequently, the euro area countries agreed that the loss of the exchange rate tool meant that they would need to make greater efforts to control their government spending and their government budgets in order to restrain inflationary pressures and to promote similar economic performance among countries that have widely disparate economies. As a result, the euro area countries adopted budget rules as a component of their common policy approach.

As the Pact took effect in 1999, EU members began criticizing the rules-based approach of the Pact for being too stringent and they questioned whether the rules could be enforced. In 2003, the weaknesses of the Pact were exposed when the European Council voted not to apply the punitive procedures under the Excessive Deficit Procedure to France and Germany, which had experienced rising levels of government debt. Some EU members argued that the Pact focused too heavily on the rules-based percentage guidelines associated with the Pact without regard for the circumstances under which a government's level of debt or its deficit spending may rise, for instance as a result of a temporary increase in government spending to counter an economic downturn.[14]

The EU experience with the Pact demonstrates the policy tradeoffs that generally are involved in adopting such programs. In order to have a fiscal consolidation program be effective, the program needs to have stringent rules and penalties for violating the rules. At the same time, the current economic recession and financial crisis have demonstrated that policymakers need some flexibility and discretion in implementing budget rules in order to adjust the policy mix and generally to respond to differences in economic conditions. A fiscal deficit during periods of economic recession or very slow growth, for instance, likely would require a different policy prescription than one that arises during periods of strong economic growth when revues would be high and payments made through automatic stabilizers would be low.

In 2005, the EU members adopted a number of changes to the Stability and Growth Pact. These changes shifted the enforcement of the Pact from a rules-based regime to one based more on a set of principles with more latitude for discretion in enforcing the corrective requirements. In the area of prevention, the modified Pact provides for each EU member to develop its own medium-term objectives to bring its deficit spending and its debt level into compliance based on the unique economic conditions of each member. The modified Pact also relaxes the annual deficit targets as Members move their budget balances into compliance and the Pact factors in the effects of cyclical economic activity. The corrective measures also were modified in a number of important ways. The changes allow Members to avoid the corrective measures if their annual fiscal deficit is above 3% of GDP if they can demonstrate that the deficit is caused by "exceptional and temporary" circumstances. In addition, members can argue that their budget deficit should be exempt from the penalties of the Excessive Deficit Procedure if they can demonstrate that the deficit is the result of "other relevant factors." Among the other relevant factors that are listed as fiscal expenditures are: 1) officially sponsored research and development; 2) European policy goals; 3) support for international objectives; 4) capital expenditure programs; 5) pension reform; 6) fiscal consolidation programs; and 7) high contributions to EU-wide initiatives.

In 2008 as the financial crisis was unfolding, EU members were asked to provide a fiscal stimulus to their economies in ways that would comply with the Stability and Growth Pact. These efforts were part of a $256 billion Economic Recovery Plan[15] proposed by the European Commission to fund cross-border projects, including investments in clean energy and upgraded telecommunications infrastructure. In order to comply with the Stability and Growth Pact, the EU asked its members to make their fiscal stimulus plans timely, temporary, and targeted, so they would not have a permanent impact on tax rates or on spending commitments beyond that necessary to counter the effects of the two crises. As a result, each EU member was asked to contribute an amount equivalent to 1.5% of their GDP to boost consumer demand. In addition, members were tasked to invest in such capital projects as energy efficient equipment in order to create jobs and to save energy, invest in environmentally clean technologies to convert such sectors as construction and automobiles to low-carbon sectors, and to invest in infrastructure and communications. This plan also proposed official support measures to increase the rate of employment and to focus investments on such high technology sectors as telecommunications and environmentally safe technologies.

CONCLUSIONS

Financial markets and policymakers are growing increasingly concerned over the high level of deficit spending and the growing amount of government debt among a large number of advanced and developing economies. Unlike previous bouts with rising government deficits in developing countries, most of the current increase in government spending does not reflect out of control spending, but represents a calculated response to a severe economic downturn and a global financial crisis. In general, the two crises have affected the balance sheets of the central governments in three broad areas: 1) special fiscal measures to address the financial crisis; 2) discretionary fiscal stimulus measures to spur economic growth; and 3) a surge in non- discretionary spending and a loss of tax revenue. As a result of these factors, the financial crisis has undermined the effectiveness of budget rules as government budgets are affected by large or prolonged internal or external shocks. Most estimates indicate that such deficits will stabilize in 2010, but will not decline appreciably for some time after that. On balance, losses in tax revenue and an increase in spending associated with fiscal stimulus measures to counter the economic recession and the financial crisis are expected to have a relatively equal negative impact on the budget balances of the developed countries.

One approach most developed countries have used to address government budget deficits has been to adopt a budget rule. In general, most developed countries have at some time adopted budget rules to restrict the amount of deficit spending to a specified percent of GDP and to constrain the overall level of the central government's debt. One common feature of these rules, however, is that most of them were applied for a relatively short period of time. In contrast, members of the EU have adopted both short-term, country-specific budget rules, and long-term EU-wide budget rules. Academic studies seem to indicate that the more successful budget efforts combined rules to balance the budget with requirements to reduce expenditures. In developing such budget rules, policymakers are caught between designing rules that are enforceable, but inflexible, versus rules that are flexible and responsive to discretion, but less enforceable.

For national policymakers, the rising budget deficits and nascent economic recovery present a challenging policy mix. Various governments have budget rules in place to limit the budget deficits, but the necessity of continuing to provide stimulus to their economies to keep the recovery on track has put these budget rules on hold. For policymakers, the challenge is to unwind the fiscal stimulus measures that were adopted to prop up the financial sector and boost economic growth without short-circuiting the economic recovery. The strength of the economic recovery will determine the extent to which these dual policy goals are in conflict. A faster pace recovery will reduce the size of the government's budget deficits, which should work to ease the concerns of financial markets. Over the short-term, however, financial markets have displayed increased weariness over the magnitude and the pervasive nature of the deficits, especially in Europe. This could result in tighter credit and higher interest rates for all market participants. Investors are particularly concerned over the exploding government debts and public unrest in Spain, Greece, Portugal, and Ireland. Eventually, the wealthier economies of Europe, particularly France and Germany, may feel compelled to step in and provide financial assistance to the four struggling economies. This incident may well provide one more challenge to European economic integration.

End Notes

[1] *World Economic Outlook*, International Monetary Fund, October 2009.

[2] Members of the G-20 are: Argentina, Australia, Brazil, Canada, China, France, Germany, India, Indonesia, Italy, Japan, Mexico, Russia, Saudi Arabia, South Africa, South Korea, Turkey, the United Kingdom, the United States, and the European Union.

[3] *The State of Public Finances: Outlook and Medium-Term Policies After the 2008 Crisis*, International Monetary Fund, March 6, 2009.

[4] *BIS Quarterly Review*, The Bank for International Settlements, March 2010, p.1.

[5] Faiola, Anthony, Debt Concerns Weigh on Europe, *The Washington Post*, February 6, 2010, p. A1.

[6] The sixteen members of the Eurozone are: Austria, Belgium, Cyprus, Finland, France, Germany, Greece, Ireland, Italy, Luxembourg, Malta, Netherlands, Portugal, Slovakia, Slovenia, and Spain.

[7] *OECD Economic Outlook*, Organization for Economic Cooperation and Development, June 2009, p. 212.

[8] Haugh, David, Patrice Ollivaud, and David Turner, *The Macroeconomic Consequences of Banking Crises in OECD Countries*, Organization for Economic Cooperation and Development, March 6, 2009.

[9] Kumar, Manmohan S., Daniel Leigh, and Alexander Plekhanov, *Fiscal Adjustments: Determinants and Macroeconomic Consequences,* International Monetary Fund, IMF Working Paper WP/07/178, July 1007, p. 22.

[10] Guichard, Stephanie, Mike Kennedy, Echkard Wursel, and Christophe Andre, *What Promotes Fiscal Consolidation: OECD Country Experiences*, the Organization for Economic Cooperation and Development, Working Paper No. 553, May 28, 2007, p. 7.

[11] Ibid., p. 10.

[12] Guichard, Stephanie, Mike Kennedy, Echkard Wursel, and Christophe Andre, *What Promotes Fiscal Consolidation: OECD Country Experiences*, Organization for Economic Cooperation and Development, May 28, 2007.

[13] Public Finances in the EMU 2009, p. 30.

[14] Beetsma, Roel M.W.J., and Xavier Debrun, *Implementing the Stability and Growth Pact: Enforcement and Procedural Flexibility*, IMF Working Paper WP/05/59, International Monetary Fund, March 2005.

[15] *A European Economic Recovery Plan*: Communication From the Commission to the European Council, Commission of the European Communities, COM(2008) 800 final, November 26, 2008. The full report is available at: http://ec.europa.eu/commission_barroso/president

In: International Debt in Individual Countries ISBN: 978-1-61761-787-4
Editors: Anthony L. Montefusco

Chapter 2

FREQUENTLY ASKED QUESTIONS ABOUT IMF INVOLVEMENT IN THE EUROZONE DEBT CRISIS

Rebecca M. Nelson, Dick K. Nanto, Jonathan E. Sanford and Martin A. Weiss

SUMMARY

On May 2, 2010, the Eurozone member states and the International Monetary Fund (IMF) announced an unprecedented €110 billion (about $145 billion) financial assistance package for Greece. The following week, on May 9, 2010, EU leaders announced that they would make an additional €500 billion (about $636 billion) in financial assistance available to vulnerable European countries, and suggested that the IMF could contribute up to an additional €220 billion to €250 billion (about $280 billion to $318 billion). This chapter answers frequently asked questions about IMF involvement in the Eurozone debt crisis.

For more information on the Greek debt crisis, see CRS Report R4 1167, *Greece's Debt Crisis: Overview, Policy Responses, and Implications*, coordinated by Rebecca M. Nelson.

Background on the Eurozone and the IMF

What is the Eurozone?

The Eurozone refers to the group of European Union (EU) countries that use the euro (€) as their national currency. The euro was introduced in 1999 as an accounting currency and in 2002 as physical currency in circulation. The Eurozone originally included 11 countries and has since expanded to 16 countries. Greece joined the Eurozone in 2000. Currently, the countries in the Eurozone include Austria, Belgium, Cyprus, Finland, France, Germany, Greece, Ireland, Italy, Luxembourg, Malta, the Netherlands, Portugal, Slovakia, Slovenia, and Spain.

The EU has 27 member states. Denmark, Sweden, and the United Kingdom are members of the EU that have opted out of joining the Eurozone. All recent entrants to the EU, including Bulgaria, the Czech Republic, Estonia, Hungary, Latvia, Lithuania, Poland, and Romania, are required to adopt the euro as their national currency as soon as possible, but must meet certain economic policy targets before they are eligible. Budgetary discipline is one of the criteria for joining the euro. Under the Treaty on European Union, commonly referred to as the Maastricht Treaty, EU member states are required to stay below a government budget deficit ceiling of 3% of GDP and external debt ceiling of 60% of GDP. Enforcement by EU authorities has been weak, however, and many governments have exceeded these ceilings. When the euro was introduced, some raised concerns about the viability of an economic union that has a common monetary policy but diverse national fiscal policies.

What is the IMF?

The International Monetary Fund (IMF) is an international financial institution that was created after World War II to promote exchange rate and monetary stability. The founders aimed to avoid the beggar-thy-neighbor exchange rate policies and banking instability that deepened the Depression during the 1930s and the lack of any international mechanism for setting standards or coordinating policy. The IMF has changed over time as the world financial system has evolved. It now provides more technical assistance to member countries on banking and finance issues. However, its principal function is still one of lending money and encouraging reform to help countries deal with balance-of-payments and financial crises. The main concern is the possible contagion effects that might bring down other countries if a crisis in a specific country is not addressed.

The IMF is owned by its member countries, whose votes are proportional to the amount of money they have subscribed to help fund its operations. The IMF funds its own internal budget from income earned through its lending program. The disbursements for IMF loans are generally conditional on the borrower country implementing reforms. Loans are generally disbursed in phases ("tranches") in order to encourage compliance with loan conditions. If conditions are not met, funds are not disbursed. The IMF charges its borrowers a rate of interest roughly equivalent to the price that major governments around the world pay to borrow funds, and it pays its member countries interest when it uses their quota resources to fund its loans. Disbursements for its regular loans, called Stand-By Arrangements (SBA), are repayable in five to eight years. Repayments for some of the IMF 's more specialized programs may occur over a longer period of time. Until the mid-1970s, developed countries were frequent borrowers from the IMF. Since then, developing countries (particularly emerging markets) have been the principal borrowers. However, during the recent financial crisis, the IMF lent substantially to several of the newer members of the European Union (EU), and it has also assisted countries with advanced economies from time to time.

EUROZONE/IMF FINANCIAL ASSISTANCE PACKAGE FOR GREECE

Why did Greece Turn to the other Eurozone Member States and the IMF for Financial Assistance?

Over the past decade, Greece borrowed heavily in international capital markets to fund government budget and trade deficits. High government spending, weak revenue collection, structural rigidities, and loss of competitiveness are typically cited as major factors behind Greece's accumulation of debt. Access to capital at low interest rates after adopting the euro and weak enforcement of EU rules concerning debt and deficit ceilings may also have played a role.

Reliance on financing from international capital markets left Greece highly vulnerable to shifts in investor confidence. Investors became increasingly nervous in October 2009, when the newly elected Greek government nearly doubled the government 2009 budget deficit estimate. Over the next months, the government announced several austerity packages and had successful rounds of bond sales on international capital markets to raise needed funds. In late April 2010, when the European Union's (EU's) statistical agency, Eurostat, further revised the estimate of Greece's 2009 deficit upwards, Greek bond spreads spiked and two major credit rating agencies downgraded Greek bonds. Greece's debt crisis threatened to spread to other European countries, including Ireland, Italy, Portugal, and Spain, that may face fiscal challenges similar to Greece.

The Greek government formally requested financial assistance from the 16 countries that use the euro as their national currency (the Eurozone) and the IMF on April 23, 2010. It was hoped that the financial assistance, combined with austerity measures, would prevent the Greek government from restructuring or defaulting on its debt or, more dramatically, from abandoning the euro in favor of a national currency.

What Financial Assistance is being Provided to Greece?

On May 2, 2010, the Eurozone member states and the IMF announced a three-year, €110 billion (about $145 billion) financial assistance package for Greece.[1] This package takes the form of loans made at market-based interest rates.

Figure 1 shows the sources of funds for the financial assistance package for Greece. Eurozone countries are to contribute €80 billion (about $105 billion) in bilateral loans, pending parliamentary approval in some countries. Each of the Eurozone countries (besides Greece) has pledged a bilateral loan, with the largest bilateral loans pledged by Germany and France (about $29.3 billion and $22 billion, respectively).

The IMF is to contribute a €30 billion (about $40 billion) loan.[2] Of the total, the IMF would draw half from IMF quota resources (the financial commitment countries make to the IMF upon joining) and half from bilateral lines of credit pledged by some member countries.

It is worth noting that it is not clear how much of the €110 billion (about $145 billion) committed by the IMF and the Eurozone member states will be used by Greece.

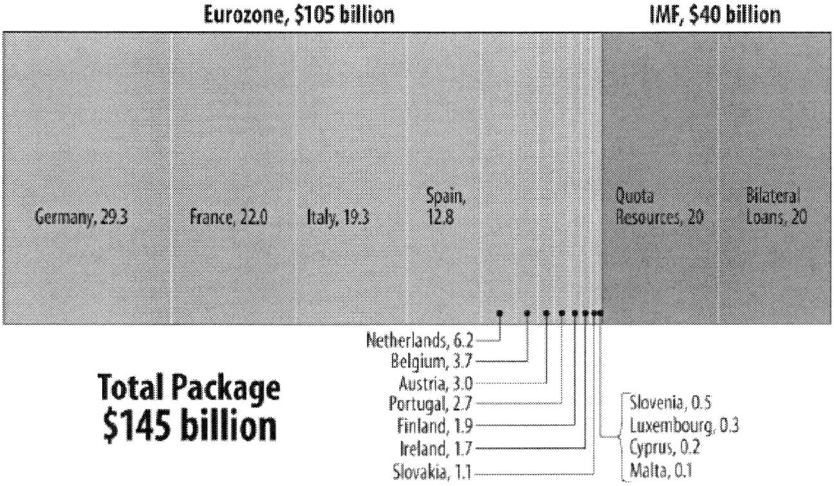

Source: Graphic prepared by CRS using data from Jan Strupczewski, "Factbox - Progress Towards Approving Emergency Loans to Greece," *Reuters*, May 6, 2010; and IMF, "Frequently Asked Questions: Greece," May 11, 2010, http://www.imf.org/external/np/exr/faq/greecefaqs.htm#q23.

Notes: Eurozone member state commitments are bilateral loans, and some commitments are subject to parliamentary approval. IMF quota resources and bilateral loans fund a Stand-By Arrangement (SBA) loan for Greece. Conversion to dollars from euros using exchange rate of €1 = $1.31 8.

Figure 1. Eurozone/IMF Financial Assistance Package for Greece Eurozone member state or IMF source of resources, Billion US$.

The money is disbursed in phases as Greece meets IMF loan conditions. If IMF officials say that Greece does not meet theseconditions, IMF disbursements will not be made. Alternatively, if creditor confidence in Greece is restored and Greece can resume selling bonds on international capital markets at reasonable interest rates, the Greek government may not need to rely on Eurozone and IMF financial commitments. On the other hand, some economists have predicted that the financial package for Greece may not be sufficient to prevent Greece from restructuring its debt and/or exiting the Eurozone.

What is the U.S. Contribution to the IMF Loan to Greece?

The IMF loan to Greece is to be financed by two different sources of money. Half of the IMF loan to Greece (about $20 billion) will be financed by IMF quota resources. IMF quotas are the financial commitments that IMF members make upon joining the IMF and are broadly based on the IMF member's relative size in the world economy. The U.S. contribution to IMF quota resources is 17%. However, we cannot infer that 17% of the IMF loan financed by IMF quota resources ($20 billion) is from the United States. Once the IMF Executive Board approves a specific loan, there is an administrative decision made by the IMF as to which countries' quotas will be tapped to fund that particular loan. The IMF does not disclose parties on individual transactions, but over time aims to provide a balanced position for all members.

The other half (about $20 billion) of the IMF loan to Greece is expected to be financed by bilateral loans. These bilateral loans will become part of the IMF's supplemental fund, the New Arrangements to Borrow (NAB), when it becomes operational. They are available now, however, before the expanded NAB goes into effect. In 2009, the United States enacted legislation to extend a line of credit worth $100 billion as part of expanding the NAB. However, because the expanded NAB is not yet operational, this $100 billion line of credit from the United States cannot be tapped for Greece's package.

The United States has never lost money on its commitment to the IMF. All U.S. financial interactions with the IMF are off-budget and, because of accounting factors, do not result in any net outlays or have any impact on the U.S. federal budget deficit.

What is the IMF's Creditor Status in its Loan to Greece?

The IMF, like the other international financial institutions, enjoys a de facto preferred creditor status; member governments grant priority to repayment of their obligations to the IMF over other creditors. In the case of the Greece loan, IMF loans would be repaid prior to all other creditors. Financing from European countries will be junior to the IMF 's loan and will have the same status as existing Greek debt.

Who Bears the Risk of the IMF's Loan to Greece?

The IMF's membership as a whole bears any risk from lending to Greece, but, in its entire history, no member of the IMF has experienced a loss from providing resources to the IMF, either by lending to the IMF or through the payment of quota subscriptions. Furthermore, member countries whose quota resources are chosen for a specific IMF loan have a claim on the IMF 's balance sheet as a whole. Thus, even if U.S. quota is drawn for the Greece loan, which may be likely, any associated risk to the IMF 's balance sheet due to the IMF loan to Greece would be shared by all IMF members. The IMF has preferred creditor status, which means that the IMF, along with other international financial institutions, is first in line to get repaid by the member country, ahead of other creditors. Occasionally countries fall into arrears with the IMF, but no member country has lost money as a result.

Only one country (Sudan) has failed to repay the IMF over a sustained period of time. The IMF absorbed that loss from its reserves or internal resources and no member country lost money as result.

What Reforms are Part of Greece's Package with the IMF?

The IMF does not disburse the full amount of its loans to governments at once. Instead, the IMF will divide the loan into tranches (French for "slice") and will only disburse the next tranche after verifying that the specified economic policy reforms have been met. Urging policy reforms in this way ensures that the loans will be repaid to the IMF, and that the required economic reforms are implemented.

The IMF program for Greece calls for substantial reductions in government spending as well as revenue increases. Overall, the package aims to reduce Greece's government budget deficit from 13.6% of GDP in 2009 to below 3% of GDP by 2014. The IMF has referred to this program as unprecedented in terms of the adjustment effort required by the government.[3] Some of the key reforms included in Greece's program with the IMF are listed below.

In the end, IMF involvement was reportedly a key condition of German Chancellor Merkel's willingness to provide financial assistance to Greece.

KEY ELEMENTS OF THE GREECE'S REFORM PACKAGE WITH THE IMF

- **Government revenues.** Revenue measures are to yield 4% of GDP through 2013 by raising the value-added tax and taxes on luxury items, tobacco, and alcohol, among other items.
- **Revenue administration and expenditure control.** The Greek government is to strengthen its tax collection and raise contributions from those who have not carried a fair share of the tax burden. It is to safeguard revenue from the largest tax payers and strengthen budget controls. The total revenue gains and expenditure savings from these structural reforms are expected to gradually total 1.8% of GDP during the program period.
- **Financial stability.** A Financial Stability Fund, funded from the external financing package, is being set up to ensure a sound level of bank equity.
- **Entitlement programs.** Government entitlement programs are to be curtailed; selected social security benefits are to be cut while maintaining benefits for the most vulnerable.
- **Pension reform.** Comprehensive pension reform is proposed, including by curtailing provisions for early retirement.
- **Structural policies.** Government to modernize public administration, strengthen labor markets and income policies, improve the business environment, and divest state enterprises.
- **Cut military spending.** The plan envisages a significant reduction in military expenditure during the period.

Source: IMF, "Europe and IMF Agree €110 Billion Financing Plan With Greece," May 2, 2010, http://www.imf.org/external/pubs/ft/ survey

Some argue that the policy reforms (conditionality) attached to an IMF loan would lend additional impetus to reform and provide both the Greek government and the EU with an outside scapegoat for pushing through politically unpopular reforms. The EU would also make policy reforms a condition of loans, but the IMF is seen as more independent than the EU and has more experience in resolving debt crises than the EU. Some have also argued that IMF participation also reportedly enabled Eurozone countries to agree more easily on the terms and conditions of the loan program than might have been the case had they had to arrange it separately.

What is Unusual about the Greece Package with the IMF?

On the one hand, the IMF loan to Greece is a standard IMF program. The IMF lends to countries facing balance-of-payment difficulties, and it is widely agreed that Greece was facing substantial balance-of-payments problems. Greece, as a member of the IMF, is entitled to draw on IMF resources, pending approval by the IMF management. The procedure by which Greece obtained its loan from the IMF was standard, as was the specific IMF loan instrument to Greece (a three- year Stand-By Arrangement [SBA]).

On the other hand, Greece's program with the IMF is unusual for two reasons. First, since the late 1970s, the IMF has not generally lent to developed countries and has never lent to a Eurozone member state since the euro was created. That said, the IMF has had programs with countries in Europe before but, with the exception of Iceland's IMF program in 2008, IMF involvement in Europe has not been recent. For example, in the 1970s, the IMF had programs with the United Kingdom, Spain, and Italy. In the early 1980s, the IMF also had a program with Portugal.

Second, Greece's program with the IMF is unusual for its relative magnitude. The IMF has general limits on the amount it will lend to a country either through an SBA or Extended Fund Facility (EFF), which is similar to an SBA but for countries facing longer-term balance-ofpayments problems. The IMF's guidelines for limits on the size of loans for SBAs and EFFs are 200% of a member's quota annually and 600% of a member's quota cumulatively.[4] IMF quotas are the financial commitments that IMF members make upon joining the IMF and are broadly based on the IMF member's relative size in the world economy. In "exceptional" situations, the IMF reserves the right to lend in excess of these limits, and has done so in the past. The IMF 's loan to Greece is indeed exceptional access at 3,200% of Greece's IMF quota and is the largest access of IMF quota resources granted to an IMF member country.[5] Previously, the largest access had been granted to South Korea during the Asian financial crisis in the 1 990s, at nearly 2,000% of Korea's quota resources.

What other Policy Options did Greece have?

Greece is addressing its sovereign debt crisis through a mix of fiscal austerity measures and structural reforms to improve the competitiveness of its industries. Many believe that the measures being implemented by the Greek government will lead to low levels of economic growth and increase unemployment. Financial assistance from the other Eurozone member states and the IMF is allowing the adjustment to take place over a longer period of time.

Greece could have addressed its sovereign debt crisis by restructuring its debt or by leaving the Eurozone. Some economists believe that Greece may still be forced to pursue one or both of these policy options. Debt restructuring, for example by negotiating with its bond holders to extend the maturity of Greek bonds or to take a cut in debt repayments, would alleviate immediate pressure on the Greek government's debt payments. However, debt restructuring could accelerate the contagion of the crisis to other Eurozone countries, as well as hinder Greece's ability to regain access to capital markets in the future.

Greece could also have addressed its sovereign debt crisis by leaving the Eurozone. This would require abandoning the euro, issuing a new national currency, and allowing the new national currency to depreciate against the euro. The Greek government would also probably have to put restrictions on bank withdrawals to prevent a run on the banks during the transition from the euro to a national currency. It is thought by some that a new national currency depreciated against the euro would spur export-led growth in Greece and offset the contractionary effects of fiscal austerity. Since Greece's debt is denominated in euros, however, leaving the Eurozone in favor of a depreciated national currency would raise the value of Greece's debt in terms of national currency and put pressure on other vulnerable European countries. Additionally, some argue that a Greek departure from the Eurozone would be economically catastrophic, lead to contagion to other European countries facing similar circumstances, and have serious ramifications for political relations among the European states and future European integration. Eurozone/IMF Financial Assistance Package for other Eurozone Countries.

Why did the Eurozone Leaders Pledge Support to other Eurozone Countries?

Despite the enactment of the Eurozone/IMF assistance package for Greece, investor concerns about the sustainability of Eurozone debt deepened during the first week of May 2010. Driven down by such fears, global stock markets plunged sharply on May 6, 2010, and the euro fell to a 15-month low against the dollar. Seeking to head off the possibility of contagion to countries such as Portugal and Spain, EU finance ministers agreed to a broader €500 billion (about $636 billion) "European Financial Stabilization Mechanism" on May 9, 2010. Some analysts assert that such a bold, large-scale move had become an urgent imperative for the EU in order to break the momentum of a gathering European financial crisis. Investors initially reacted positively to the announcement of the new agreement, with global stock markets rebounding on May 10, 2010, to regain the sharp losses of the week before.

What Financial Assistance has been Pledged by the EU and the IMF?

The bulk of the European Financial Stabilization Mechanism package consists of a "Special Purpose Vehicle" under which Eurozone countries could make available bilateral loans and government-backed loan guarantees totaling up to €440 billion (about $560 billion) to stabilize the euro area. The agreement, which expires after three years, requires parliamentary ratification in some Eurozone countries. The mechanism additionally allows the European Commission to raise money on capital markets and loan up to €60 billion (about $76 billion) to Eurozone states. Previously, such a procedure could only be applied to non-Eurozone members of the EU, and was used after the global financial crisis to improve the balance-of-payments situations of Latvia, Hungary, and Romania. Lastly, the European Central Bank (ECB) may take on a more significant new role; if necessary to increase market confidence, the ECB can now buy member state bonds, an activity in which it has not previously engaged.

EU leaders announced the European Financial Stabilization Mechanism and suggested the IMF could contribute up to an additional €220 billion to €250 billion (about $280 billion to about $318 billion). This is in line with the Greece package, where the Eurozone states contributed roughly two-thirds and the IMF one-third of the total. IMF Managing Director John Lipsky reportedly later clarified the news reports about the IMF contribution to the European Financial Stabilization Mechanism, saying that these pledges were "illustrative" of the support that the IMF could provide.[6] Reportedly, Lipsky reiterated that the IMF only provides loans to countries that have requested IMF assistance and that Greece is the only Eurozone country to date that has requested IMF assistance.[7]

What is the Role of the U.S. Federal Reserve?[8]

On May 9, 2010, the Federal Reserve (Fed) announced the re-establishment of temporary reciprocal currency agreements, known as swap lines, with the European Central Bank, Bank of Canada, the Bank of England, Bank of Japan, and the Swiss National Bank.[9] Under these agreements the Fed swaps dollars for foreign currencies for a fixed period of time with interest being paid to the Fed on the dollar amounts involved. The swaps are repaid at the exchange rate at the time of the original swap, meaning that these repayment amounts are not affected by changes in exchange rates while the swap is outstanding. Thus, there is no exchange rate risk and, except in the unlikely event that the borrowing country's currency becomes unconvertible in foreign exchange markets, there is also no credit risk involved for the Fed. The highest recent outstanding amount was approximately $583 billion in December 2008.

The swap lines are intended to provide liquidity to banks in non-domestic denominations. For example, many European banks have borrowed in dollars to finance dollar-denominated transactions, such as the purchase of U.S. assets. Normally, foreign banks could finance their dollar-denominated borrowing through the private inter-bank lending market. Such private lending markets, however, have greatly diminished, if not disappeared, in periods of crisis over the past few years. Thus, central banks at home and abroad have taken a much larger role in directly providing liquidity to banks. The swap lines with the Federal Reserve provide foreign central banks with a source of dollar liquidity should such liquidity be needed.

IMF RESOURCES AND CONGRESS'S ROLE

How Much Money does the IMF have to Lend?

In April 2009, the G-20 Leaders and the International Monetary and Financial Committee agreed to increase the resources available to the IMF through immediate bilateral financing from members and to subsequently expand the NAB and make it more flexible. [10] Resources from new bilateral contributions are available and being drawn on for current IMF programs. The expanded NAB is not yet operational.

As of May 6, 2010, the IMF has about $272 billion dollars immediately available to lend.[11] This figure is the IMF 's one-year forward commitment capacity (FCC), which measures the IMF 's ability to make new non-concessional resources available to members over the next 12 months. This includes, among other sources, unused quota resources, currently active bilateral loans to the IMF from several advanced economies, and note purchase agreements with three large emerging- market countries.[12]

What is the Expanded New Arrangements to Borrow (NAB)?

Created in the late 1 990s, the New Arrangements to Borrow (NAB) is a supplemental fund that the IMF can use to finance loans under exceptional circumstances that pose a threat to the international monetary system. The G-20 proposed in April 2009 that the existing NAB be expanded and made more flexible in light of increased demand for IMF assistance. Following a year of negotiations on the design and operations of the expanded NAB, the IMF Executive Board adopted a proposal on April 12, 2010, by which the NAB would be expanded to about $550 billion, with the addition of 13 new participating countries.[13] The U.S. commitment to the expanded NAB is $100 billion and the necessary authorizations and appropriations were enacted in FY2009.[14]

Despite U.S. approval of its contribution to the expanded NAB in FY2009, the expanded NAB is not yet operational and U.S. resources pledged to it cannot be activated until a sufficient number of current and new participants provide formal consent. Participating in the expanded NAB involves domestic approval procedures in many countries, including legislative approval before they can consent or adhere to the expanded NAB. The IMF has not published the status of NAB approvals. Once the expanded NAB becomes operational, the bilateral loan and note purchase agreements would be folded into the NAB.

If and when the expanded NAB becomes operational, the process for approving use of NAB resources will change. Under the current NAB, NAB resources can be used if approval is secured from: (1) NAB participants representing 80% of total NAB credit arrangements; and (2) members of the IMF Executive Board representing 50% of the voting share. Use of NAB resources is currently considered on a loan-by-loan basis. Under the current NAB, the United States does not have sufficient voting power to unilaterally veto use of NAB resources.

Under the expanded NAB, the NAB would be activated for a period of time (up to six months). During this "activation period," calls can be made on the NAB without additional consent by the NAB participants or the IMF Executive Board. To activate the expanded NAB, it will be necessary to secure approval from: (1) NAB participants representing 85% of total NAB credit arrangements eligible to vote; and (2) members of the IMF Executive Board representing 50% of the voting share. Under the expanded and modified NAB, the United States will be able to unilaterally veto activating the NAB. If the expanded and modified NAB is activated, however, the United States will not be able to dictate or vote on which loans approved by the IMF Executive Board can be financed with NAB resources during the activation period.

How does the United States Provide Money to the IMF?

Since 1945, the United States has subscribed about $55 billion as its quota in the IMF. The Bretton Woods Agreements Act provides that, unless Congress agrees by law, the United States cannot provide money or subscribe resources to the IMF. Over the years, Congress has passed several laws authorizing the Secretary of the Treasury to agree that the United States will participate in IMF funding agreements and authorizing and appropriating the necessary funds. Congress has used a variety of budgetary arrangements to provide this money. A country's quota in the IMF is a line of credit, which is available to the IMF upon request when it needs money to fund a loan to one of its borrower countries. When the IMF wishes to draw against the U.S. quota, it asks the New York Federal Reserve Bank to transfer money from the Treasury Department's account to its account so it will have the resources necessary for that loan. The IMF usually draws on the resources of several countries to fund its loans. U.S. financial relations with the IMF are off-budget. For accounting reasons, payments to the IMF from U.S. quota resources have no outlay effect and no impact on the federal budget deficit. As loans are repaid to the IMF, it transfers the borrowed funds back to the United States. The IMF pays the United States and other countries interest on the outstanding balance whenever it uses their quota resources.

What is the Role of Congress?

Once Congress has approved U.S. participation and provided appropriated funds to back an additional U.S. subscription, it has no further role in the IMF lending process. Neither individual loans nor the IMF's ability to draw against U.S. quota resources must be approved in advance by Congress. At the time the United States subscribes to new quota resources, it may not put restrictions on the ways the IMF may use those funds, as this would violate the terms of the IMF funding agreements. Congress may enact legislation requiring the U.S. executive director at the IMF to oppose loans to specific countries or for specific purposes. However, with 16.8% of the total vote, the United States cannot by itself block approval of loans by the IMF Executive Board.

IMPLICATIONS OF THE EUROZONE DEBT CRISIS FOR THE UNITED STATES

How Strong are the Economic Ties between the United States and the EU?

The United States and the European Union (EU) economic relationship is the largest in the world—and it is growing.[15] The modern U.S.-European economic relationship has evolved since World War II, broadening as the six-member European Community expanded into the present 27- member European Union. The ties have also become more complex and interdependent, covering a growing number and type of trade, investment, and financial activities.

In 2008, $1,571.2 billion flowed between the United States and the EU on the current account, the most comprehensive measure of U.S. trade flows. The EU as a unit is the largest merchandise trading partner of the United States. In 2008, the EU accounted for $274.5 billion of total U.S. exports (or 21.1%) and for $367.9 billion of total U.S. imports (or 17.5%) for a U.S. trade deficit of $93.4 billion. The EU is also the largest U.S. trade partner when trade in services is added to trade in merchandise, accounting for $198.3 billion (or 36.4% of the total in U.S. services exports) and $152.1 billion (or 37.6% of total U.S. services imports) in 2008. In addition, in 2008, a net $148.2 billion flowed from U.S. residents to EU countries into direct investments, while a net $181.1 billion flowed from EU residents to direct investments in the United States.[16]

What is the Exposure of U.S. Banks to Vulnerable European Countries?

This table shows only direct bank lending. What is generally not known is the exposure of U.S. financial institutions through issuance of credit default swaps based on Greek sovereign debt. The effect of credit default swaps could be to lower U.S. bank exposure to sovereign debt by offsetting U.S. bank liabilities or to raise U.S. bank exposure to sovereign debt if U.S. banks sold credit protection.[17]

Table 1. U.S. Banking Exposure to Greece, Ireland, Italy, Portugal, and Spain Amounts Outstanding, Billions of US$, End-2009 Quarter 4

Country	Amount
Greece	16.6
Ireland	58.6
Italy	53.8
Portugal	5.0
Spain	52.7
Total	**186.7**

Source: Bank for International Settlements (BIS), "Consolidated International Claims of BIS Reporting Banks," provisional data for end-2009 Q4 (most recent data available), Table 9B: Consolidated Foreign Claims of Reporting Banks - Immediate Borrower Basis, http://www.bis.org/statistics

Notes: Provisional data.

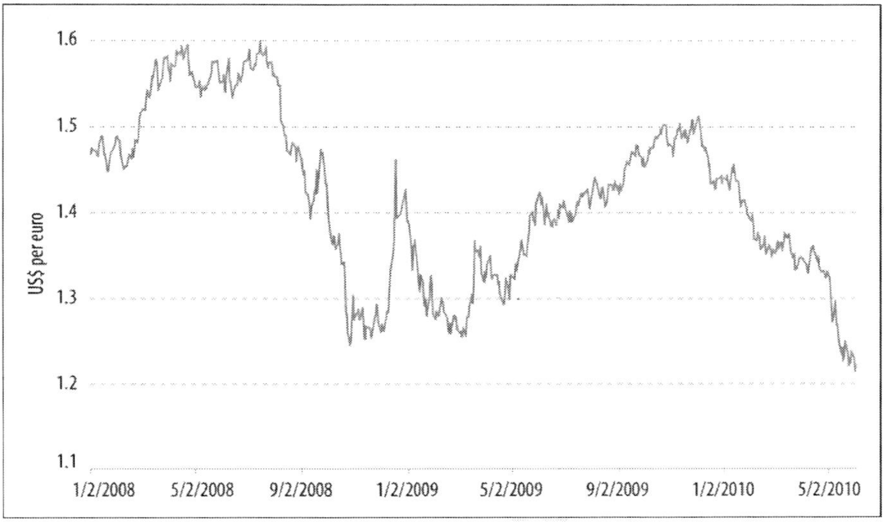

Source: European Central Bank (ECB).

Figure 2. US$/Euro Exchange Rate, January 2008 – May 2010.

How has Financial Instability in the Eurozone affected the Value of the Dollar?

Some expect that if investors lose confidence in the future of the Eurozone, and more current account adjustment is required for the Eurozone as a whole, the value of the euro will weaken. Already, the euro has depreciated in recent months against the U.S. dollar (**Figure 2**), falling by 19% between December 12, 2009, and June 2, 2010 (from 1.51 $/€ to 1.22 $/€). A weaker euro would likely lower U.S. exports to the Eurozone and increase U.S. imports from the Eurozone, widening the U.S. trade deficit. On the other hand, it will make purchases and U.S. investments in Eurozone countries cheaper in dollar terms.

Since the Chinese renminbi has been tied to the value of the dollar, when the dollar appreciates against the euro, the renminbi also does so. This raises the price of Chinese exports to the Eurozone and lowers the price of European exports to China. This exchange rate effect not only affects China's trade with Europe, but it could make the United States a more attractive market for products from China.

How Has the Eurozone Instability Affected U.S. Interest Rates?

Since U.S. Treasury securities are considered to be a safe haven for investors during times of economic turmoil, the immediate effect of the Greek crisis was for investors to reduce their exposure to euro-denominated investments, particularly those issued by Greece, and invest some of those funds in U.S. Treasuries. This caused a greater inflow of funds into the United States and caused the yield on 10-year Treasury notes to fall by about one-third of a percentage point (see **Figure 3**). If these lower interest rates persist, U.S. borrowers, including the U.S. Treasury and those seeking mortgages, will benefit. In June 2010, some long-term mortgage interest rates had fallen to as low as 4.25%. For those who rely on interest bearing assets for income, however, lower interest rates reduce the yields they receive on bonds and other securities. In the future, though, if Eurozone member states default on loans to leveraged banks, global credit markets may shrink by a multiple of the losses as banks deleverage.[18] If this occurs, global interest rates, including those in the United States, could rise. [19]

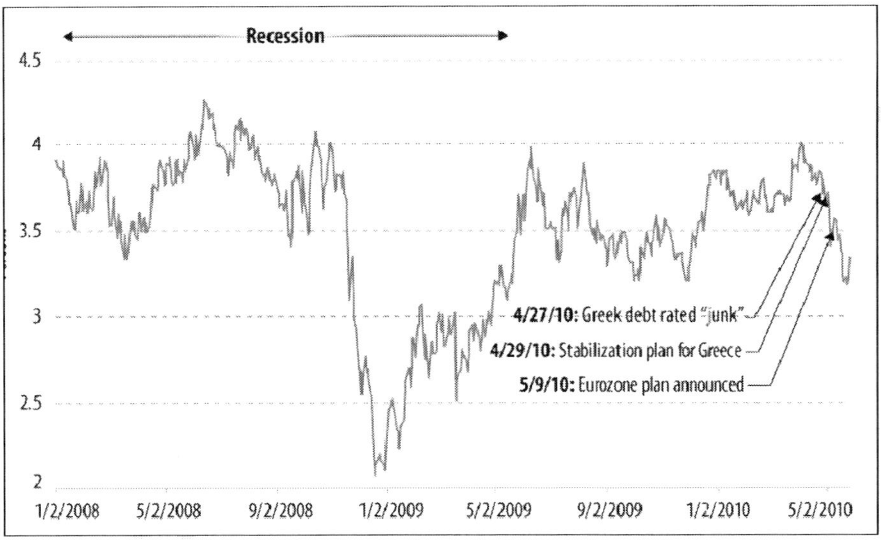

Source: CRS with data from U.S. Treasury.

Figure 3. Yields (Interest Rates) on U.S. 10-year Treasury Notes.

How will U.S. Economic Growth be Affected?

The Eurozone instability is affecting the U.S. economy through several economic and financial linkages. The first is in capital flows into the "safe haven" of U.S. Treasury securities and causing lower interest rates as addressed above. The second is in international trade flows. Slower growth in the Eurozone likely will lead to lower U.S. exports there, while the fall in the value of the euro may further reduce the quantity of U.S. exports to the Eurozone but increase U.S. imports from Europe and travel expenditures there. Slower growth in the Eurozone also is reducing demand for petroleum and lowering the price of oil and other commodities. This will tend to reduce the U.S. import bill for petroleum and tend to increase consumer confidence in the United States. The Eurozone instability, however, also has increased the risk level with respect to sovereign and other debt and has increased volatility in stock markets. While such volatility in the short-term may not affect the overall level of consumption and investment in the United States, a large drop in equity values may reduce consumption through the wealth effect as stockholders see their wealth levels shrink and attempt to save more. Corporations also may find that raising funds for investments through new offerings of stock becomes more difficult.

Figure 4 shows the amount that real U.S. gross domestic product (GDP) has changed between first quarter 2009 to first quarter 2010. During this time, real GDP increased by $329.3 billion. This consisted of an increase in consumption of $163.5 billion, an increase in investment of $119.3 billion, an increase in net exports of $19.5 billion, and an increase in government expenditures of $38.1 billion.

How will a drop in interest rates and price for petroleum combined with increased risk and a weaker euro affect household consumption, the largest component in GDP? Economists expect that lower interest rates will provide a further boost to pent-up demand for consumer durables, the purchase of which tended to be postponed during the recession. Consumption is expected to increase in line with GDP. Investment, both by businesses in new plant and equipment and households in residential structures, is a key to U.S. recovery. As can be seen in **Figure 4**, the increase in U.S. investment over the past year has been in inventory accumulation as businesses restocked shelves in anticipation of rising sales. Growth in investments in plant and equipment and in housing has been negative. Lower interest rates provide a positive boost to investments in general, but business expectations of less export demand from Europe and increased risk of another global slowdown in growth may work to curtail new investments in production capacity. As for trade, the drop in the value of the euro and weakened demand in the Eurozone are likely to increase the U.S. trade deficit beyond that expected as U.S. consumption of imports rises. With the exception of lower interest rates on borrowing, government spending, particularly at the state and local level, does not appear to be significantly affected by the Eurozone instability.

The combined effect of these positive and negative forces on U.S. growth is difficult to ascertain, but assuming that the crisis is contained, the net effect arguably will be not large and more negative than positive. IHS Global Insight stated that it thinks "the fallout from the Greek crisis for the United States is likely to be relatively small, mostly in the form of loss of competitiveness for U.S. exporters relative to a euro that should remain weak for the foreseeable future." It expects that the Eurozone crisis "will dent the U.S. recovery, but not derail it" and expects the growth rate of U.S. GDP to fall from 3% in first quarter 2010 and about 4% in second quarter of 2010 into the 2.5–3.0% range during the second half of 2010.[20] (The U.S. GDP contracted by 2.4% in 2009.) The Economist Intelligence Unit expects U.S. growth to be 3.3% in 2010.[21]

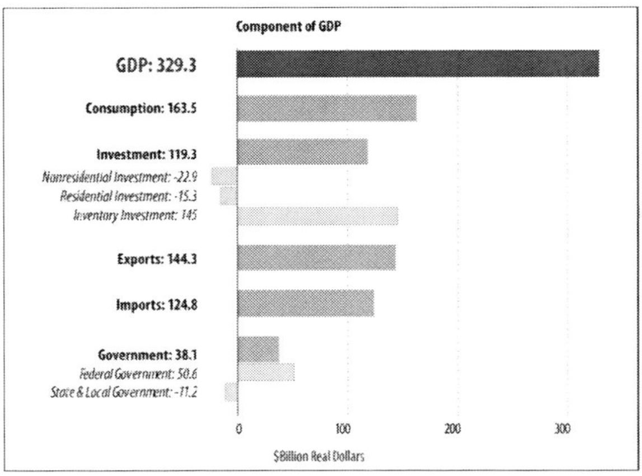

Source: Congressional Research Service with data from U.S. Department of Commerce via IHS Global Insight.

Notes: In billions of chained 2005 dollars, seasonally adjusted. GDP equals consumption plus investment plus exports minus imports plus government spending. Subcategories for investment (non-residential, residential, and inventory) and government spending (federal and state and local) are listed. Numbers may not add due to statistical discrepancies.

Figure 4. Amount of Change in U.S. Real Gross Domestic Product by Component From First Quarter 2009 to First Quarter 2010.

If, however, the Greek debt crisis is not contained and spreads to countries, such as Spain and Portugal, the effect on the United States could be considerably larger.

How do U.S. Government Budget Deficit and External Debt Levels Compare to those in Vulnerable European Countries?

Some are concerned that Greece's debt crisis foreshadows the United States' future. It is important to note that the sustainability of a government's debt depends on a host of different factors, such as the flexibility of the exchange rate, the currency in which the government has borrowed, and when the debt is falling due, among others. What may be sustainable for a particular government in a particular time may not be true for other governments. Some have suggested, for example, that although the U.S. budget deficit situation is similar to those in vulnerable European countries, the U.S. fiscal position may be stronger than these other countries because, for example, the United States has a floating exchange rate, the dollar is an international reserve currency, the U.S. overall level of debt (as a percentage of GDP) is lower, and economic growth is (albeit slowly) returning in the United States.[22] The United States is also considered a safe haven for investments, making U.S. bonds attractive on private international capital markets and making it easier for the U.S. government to rollover its debt.

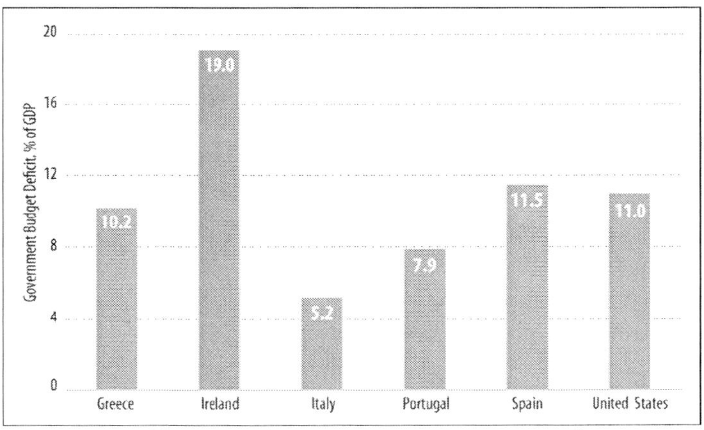

Source: Economist Intelligence Unit (EIU) Country Reports, April 2010.

Figure 5. Government Budget Deficits, 2010 Forecasts % of GDP.

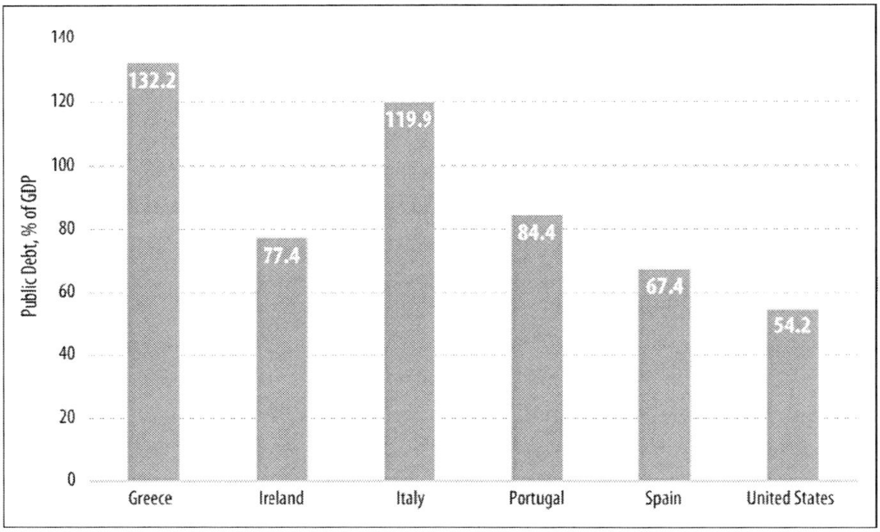

Source: Economist Intelligence Unit (EIU) Country Reports, April 2010.
Notes: Forecasts. Net public debt for Portugal and the United States.

Figure 6. Public Debt, 2010 Forecasts % of GDP.

LEGISLATIVE DEVELOPMENTS

Has Congress Adopted any Legislation in Light of the IMF Loan to Greece?

S.Amdt. 3986

On May 17, 2010, the Senate adopted (94-0) an amendment (S.Amdt. 3986) to S. 3217, the Restoring Financial Stability Act of 2010, introduced by Senator John Cornyn. The Senate passed its version of the financial regulatory reform bill (H.R. 4173), which included S.Amdt. 3986 on May 20, 2010. Conference negotiations between the House and the Senate are expected to begin shortly.

The amendment, titled "Restrictions on Use of Federal Funds to Finance Bailouts of Foreign Governments," directs the U.S. Executive Director (USED) at the IMF to evaluate any IMF loan to a country where the public debt exceeds the gross domestic product (GDP), determine and certify to

Congress whether the loan will be repaid, and use the voice and vote of the United States to oppose such IMF loans.

As written, the impact of the loan is unclear. On one hand, there is a strong record of countries repaying their loans to the IMF. The IMF is the senior creditor in debt situations and as such will be repaid before first other creditors are paid. Only three countries, Somalia, Sudan, and Zimbabwe, are currently in arrears to the IMF, and no member country has experienced a loss from providing resources to the Fund. On the other hand, the amendment appears to requires U.S. officials to have more certain knowledge about the future than is possible. Since it is impossible for the U.S. Executive Director to determine and certify to Congress whether an IMF loan will be repaid prior to the loan being made, it is unclear whether the United States would be required to oppose all future IMF loans to countries where public debt exceeds GDP. By itself, U.S. opposition to an IMF loan is not sufficient to prevent the loan from being approved by the Executive Board.

Large IMF packages to developed countries appear to be the Amendment's focus of concern. However, the provision would apply to all countries where public debt exceeds GDP and this may inadvertently require the United States to oppose IMF loans to other heavily-indebted countries. As of 2009, nine countries had public debt burdens greater than their GDP.[23] Several low income countries are near that level and might exceed it if their GDP levels shrank in the midst of a financial crisis that would prompt them to seek IMF assistance.

What Other Legislation Prompted by the IMF Loan to Greece is Congress Considering?

Three pieces of legislation have been introduced to address issues arising from the IMF loan to Greece. Two would seek to block any use of IMF resources, including those from the expanded NAB, to fund loans to EU member countries. The third would express opposition to any use of U.S.-provided funds to help support assistance under the proposed EU stability plan.

H.R. 5299 and S. 3383

On May 13, 2010, Representative Mike Pence introduced H.R. 5299, a bill titled the "European Bailout Protection Act." Senator Jim DeMint introduced a companion bill, S. 3383, on May 18, 2010. Sec. 2 would require the Secretary of the Treasury to oppose any activation of the expanded New Arrangements to Borrow (NAB) facility that would fund directly or indirectly an IMF loan to a member country of the European Union if it or any other member of the EU has a public debt-to-GDP ratio greater than 60%. Sec. 3 would direct the Secretary to instruct the USED at the IMF to oppose any assistance directly or indirectly to an EU member if any other EU member had a debt-to-GDP ratio above that level. The bills state in their heading that the provisions are temporary, but no time limitation is provided.

Because of the size of its share, the United States can block activation of the expanded NAB facility by withholding support, if and when the expanded NAB comes into effect. This legislation would require the United States to oppose use of the NAB facility for any loans to European countries that have substantial public debts. Some suggest, however, that the legislation might also have unintended effects. For example, if this legislation had been in effect last year, the United States would have had to oppose all IMF loans to post-communist countries of Central and Eastern Europe that are members of the EU, even though most analysts agree that excessive levels of public indebtedness were not the source of their difficulties.

The bills seem to presume that the expanded NAB resources will be activated on a country-bycountry basis and therefore loans to European countries can be blocked while loans to other countries may be approved. IMF member countries agreed in April 2010, however, that the expanded NAB will be activated for a set period of time (up to 6 months) and would be used to finance any applicable loans during that period. The United States has the power to prevent the NAB from being activated but it cannot veto specific borrowers. Under this legislation, the Secretary of the Treasury would need to keep the NAB shut indefinitely or risk the possibility that an EU country might unexpectedly seek to borrow during a period when the NAB has been activated.

This legislation might also prevent the existing bilateral lines of credit provided by some countries from being folded into the expanded NAB, since this would be done by reimbursing countries from the NAB for money the IMF had previously drawn from their bilateral credits. Bilateral credits were used to help fund the recent loan to Greece. Thus, if this legislation were in effect, the United States might have to oppose activation of the NAB for the purpose of reimbursing bilateral creditors for their share in the Greek loan.

H.Con.Res. 279

On May 18, 2010, Representative McMorris Rodgers introduced House Concurrent Resolution 279 (H.Con.Res. 279), a measure that would disapprove U.S. participation in any IMF funding package for the EU, unless each EU member country complies with the EU rules on deficit spending and each had a public debt-to-GDP ratio at or below 60%. The legislation seeks to discourage or prevent U.S. resources being used to help fund the European financial stability plan announced on May 9, 2010.

This legislation provides Members of Congress with a means of expressing opposition to any use of U.S. funds to help finance an IMF share in the proposed European stability plan. It currently seems unlikely, however, that IMF resources will be used to support the European plan. The IMF makes loans to individual countries and not to groups of countries, such as the EU. IMF officials also have said that the IMF has not agreed to provide any money towards the European plan. A concurrent resolution by one chamber of Congress does not have the force of law. In addition, a country's subscription to IMF quota resources is an irrevocable commitment, and legislation of this sort would not prevent the IMF from drawing on the U.S. quota or from using NAB resources to finance future IMF loans to European countries.

End Notes

1 For the Greek financial assistance package and the broader Eurozone financial assistance package, the exchange rate at the time the package was announced is used (approximately €1 = $1.31 and €1 = $1.27 respectively). Source: European Central Bank (ECB). However, currency swings are underway, and dollar conversions of data denominated in euros should be approached as estimates.

2 The loan to Greece was approved by the IMF Executive Board on May 9, 2010.

3 IMF, "Frequently Asked Questions: Greece," May 11, 2010, http://www.imf.org/external/np/exr/faq/greecefaqs.htm.

4 IMF, "IMF Quotas," March 11, 2010, http://www.imf.org/external/np/exr/facts/quotas

5 IMF, "IMF Reaches Staff-level Agreement with Greece on €30 Billion Stand-By Arrangement," press release, May 2, 2010, http://www.imf.org/external/np/sec/pr/2010/pr10176.htm.

6 Bob Davis, "IMF's Reach Spreads to Western Europe," *Wall Street Journal*, May 10, 2010.

7 Ibid.

8 Section prepared by Marc Labonte, Specialist in Macroeconomic Policy, Government and Finance Division, x7-0640. For more on the Federal Reserve, see CRS Report RL30354, *Monetary Policy and the Federal Reserve: Current Policy and Conditions*, by Marc Labonte.

9 In response to the beginnings of the recent financial crisis, similar swap lines were established in December 2007 and expired in February 2010. On the re-establishment of these lines, see Federal Reserve, "Federal Reserve, European Central Bank, Bank of Canada, Bank of

England, and Swiss National Bank Announce Reestablishment of Temporary U.S. Dollar Liquidity Swap Facilities," http://www.federalreserve.gov/newsevents/press/monetary/20100509a.htm and Federal Reserve, "FOMC Authorizes Re-establishment of Temporary U.S. Dollar Liquidity Swap Arrangement with the Bank of Japan," *http://www.federalreserve.gov/newsevents/press/monetary/20100510a.htm.*

[10] CRS Report R40578, *The Global Financial Crisis: Increasing IMF Resources and the Role of Congress*, by Jonathan E. Sanford and Martin A. Weiss.

[11] 183 billion IMF Special Drawing Rights (SDRs). See IMF Financial Activities – Update May 6, 2010, available at: http://www.imf.org/external/np/tre/activity/2010/050710.htm.

[12] The FCC is determined by the IMF's usable resources (including unused amounts under loans and note purchase agreements), plus projected loan repayments over the subsequent twelve months, less the resources that have already been committed under existing lending arrangements, less a prudential balance of 20% of the quotas of members that issue the currencies that are used in the financing of IMF transactions to "safeguard the liquidity of creditors' claims and take account of the potential erosion of the IMF's resource base." See IMF Financial Activities – Update May 6, 2010 for additional definitions.

[13] IMF Executive Board Approves Major Expansion of Fund's Borrowing Arrangements to Boost Resources for Crisis Resolution, *International Monetary Fund*, April 12, 2010.

[14] To meet the U.S. $100 billion commitment to the expanded NAB, as well as an $8 billion increase in the U.S. quota at the IMF, Congress appropriated $5 billion in the FY2009 Spring Supplemental Appropriations for Overseas Contingency Operations (P.L. 111-32).

[15] For more information, see CRS Report RL30608, *EU-U.S. Economic Ties: Framework, Scope, and Magnitude*, by William H. Cooper.

[16] Data from CRS Report RL30608, *EU-U.S. Economic Ties: Framework, Scope, and Magnitude*, by William H. Cooper.

[17] For more on credit default swaps, see CRS Report RS22932, *Credit Default Swaps: Frequently Asked Questions*, by Edward V. Murphy and Rena S. Miller.

[18] For example, see Frederic S. Mishkin, "On 'Leveraged Losses: Lessons from the Mortgage Meltdown'," Speech at the U.S. Monetary Policy Forum, New York, New York, February 29, 2008, http://www.federalreserve.gov/newsevents/speech

[19] For more on this point, see CRS Report RL34412, *Containing Financial Crisis*, by Mark Jickling.

[20] IHS Global Insight, U.*S. Executive Summary, Aegean Contagion?*, May 2010; and U.S. Economy, Economic Commentary: GDP, updated May 27, 2010, accessed June 2, 2010.

[21] Economist Intelligence Unit, *Forecast for the United States of America*, 2010. Accessed June 2, 2010.

[22] E.g., see Paul Krugman, "We're Not Greece," *New York Times*, May 13, 2011.

[23] Greece, Iceland, Italy, Jamaica, Japan, Lebanon, Singapore, Sudan and Zimbabwe, according to the Economist Intelligence Unit.

In: International Debt in Individual Countries ISBN: 978-1-61761-787-4
Editors: Anthony L. Montefusco

Chapter 3

GREECE'S DEBT CRISIS: OVERVIEW, POLICY RESPONSES, AND IMPLICATIONS

Rebecca M. Nelson, Paul Belkin and Derek E. Mix

SUMMARY

Buildup of Greece's Public Debt: Over the past decade, Greece borrowed heavily in international capital markets to fund government budget and current account deficits. The profligacy of the government, weak revenue collection, and structural rigidities in Greece's economy are typically cited as major factors behind Greece's accumulation of debt. Access to capital at low interest rates after adopting the euro and weak enforcement of EU rules concerning debt and deficit ceilings may also have played a role.

Outbreak of Greece's Debt Crisis: Reliance on financing from international capital markets left Greece highly vulnerable to shifts in investor confidence. Investors became jittery in October 2009, when the newly-elected Greek government revised the estimate of the government budget deficit to nearly double the original number. Over the next months, the government announced several austerity packages and had successful rounds of bond sales on international capital markets to raise needed funds. In late April, when Eurostat, the European Union (EU)'s statistical agency, further revised the estimate of Greece's 2009 deficit upwards, Greek bond spreads spiked and two major credit rating agencies downgraded Greek bonds.

Eurozone/IMF Financial Assistance: The Greek government formally requested financial assistance from the 16 member states of the Eurozone and the International Monetary Fund (IMF), and a €110 billion (about $145 billion) package was announced on May 2, 2010. The package aims to prevent Greece from defaulting on its debt obligations and to stem contagion of Greece's crisis to other European countries, including Portugal, Spain, Ireland, and Italy. Despite the substantial size of the package, some economists are concerned that the Eurozone/IMF package might not be enough to prevent Greece from defaulting on, or restructuring, its debt, or even from leaving the Eurozone. Greece's debt crisis threatened to widen across Europe, as bond spreads for several European countries spiked and depreciation of the euro began to accelerate.

On Sunday, May 9, 2010, EU leaders announced that they would make an additional €500 billion ($636 billion) in financial assistance available to vulnerable European countries, with the IMF contributing up to an additional €220 billion (about $280 billion) to €250 billion (about $318 billion). The same day, the European Central Bank (ECB) announced it could start buying European bonds, and the U.S. Federal Reserved also announced it would reopen currency swap lines with other major central banks, including the ECB, to help ease economic pressure. When markets opened on Monday, May 10, 2010, bond spreads in Europe dropped and the euro began to strengthen, suggesting that the package was successful in stemming the spread of Greece's crisis.

Implications for the United States: Greece's debt crisis could have several implications for the United States. First, falling investor confidence in the Eurozone has weakened the euro, which, in turn, could widen the U.S. trade deficit. Second, given the strong economic ties between the United States and the EU, financial instability in the EU could impact the U.S. economy. Third, $16.6 billion of Greece's debt is held by U.S. banks, and a Greek default would likely have ramifications for these creditors. Fourth, some have suggested that Greece's current debt crisis foreshadows what the United States could face in the future. Others argue that the analogy is weak, because the United States, unlike Greece, has a floating exchange rate and a national currency that is an international reserve currency. Fifth, the debate about imbalances within the Eurozone is similar to the debates about U.S.-China imbalances, and reiterates how, in a globalized economy, the economic policies of one country impact other countries' economies.

INTRODUCTION

Historically, financial crises have been followed by a wave of governments defaulting on their debt obligations.[1] Financial crises tend to lead to, or exacerbate, sharp economic downturns, low government revenues, widening government deficits, and high levels of debt, pushing many governments into default.[2] As recovery from the global financial crisis begins, but the global recession endures, some point to the threat of a second wave of the crisis: sovereign debt crises.[3]

Greece is currently facing such a sovereign debt crisis. On May 2, 2010, the Eurozone members and International Monetary Fund (IMF) endorsed a historic €110 billion (about $145 billion) financial package for Greece in an effort to avoid a Greek default and to stem contagion of Greece's crisis to other European countries, particularly Portugal, Spain, Ireland, and Italy.[4] On May 9, 2010, the European Union (EU) announced an additional €500 billion (about $636 billion) in financial assistance that could be made available to assist vulnerable European countries.

Greece's debt crisis has raised a host of questions about the merits of the euro and the prospects for future European monetary integration, with some calling for more integration and others less. Of heated debate, in particular, is the viability of an economic union that has a common monetary policy but diverse national fiscal policies. Some economists have suggested that Greece could benefit from abandoning the euro and issuing a new national currency, although doing so would raise the real value of Greece's external debt and possibly trigger runs on Greek banks and contagion of the crisis more broadly within the Eurozone.

The United States and the EU have strong economic ties, and a crisis in Greece that threatens to spill over to other Southern European countries could impact U.S. economic relations with the EU and the general economic recovery from the financial crisis. Additionally, the exposure of U.S. banks is estimated at $16.6 billion.[5] The Obama Administration was reportedly supportive of the EU and IMF's decision to offer financial support to Greece and other vulnerable Eurozone economies. Indeed, at least one press report indicates that Administration officials began urging their European counterparts to take decisive action to prevent the possibility of Greek default as early as February.[6] President Obama is reported to have called German Chancellor Angela Merkel and French President Nicolas Sarkozy on May 9, 2010, to encourage them to structure a broader package of financial assistance in an effort to stem possible contagion of the Greek crisis to other Eurozone

Members.[7] On May 10, 2010, the U.S. Federal Reserved reopened credit swap lines with the European Central Bank (ECB), among other major central banks, to help ease economic pressures resulting from the crisis in Europe.

Given this context, congressional interest in Greece's debt crisis is high. Greece's economic situation was a major focus of discussion during Greek Prime Minister George Papandreou's meetings with congressional leaders in a visit to Washington, DC in March 2010.[8] Numerous congressional hearings in 2010 have referenced Greece's economic situation, and the House Committee on Financial Services held a hearing on April 29, 2010, on the implications of Greece's debt crisis for credit default swaps. Given the large financial commitment of the United States to the IMF, there is also strong congressional interest in the IMF 's role in providing financial assistance to Greece.

This chapter provides an overview of the crisis; outlines the major causes of the crisis, focusing on both domestic and international factors; examines how Greece, the Eurozone members, and the IMF have responded to the crisis; and highlights the broader implications of Greece's debt crisis, including for the United States.

GREECE'S DEBT CRISIS: BACKGROUND

Buildup to the Current Crisis

During the decade preceding the global financial crisis that started in fall 2008, Greece's government borrowed heavily from abroad to fund substantial government budget and current account deficits.[9] Between 2001, when Greece adopted the euro as its currency, and 2008, Greece's reported budget deficits averaged 5% per year, compared to a Eurozone average of 2%, and current account deficits averaged 9% per year, compared to a Eurozone average of 1%. [10] In 2009, Greece's budget deficit is estimated to have been more than 13% of GDP. Many attribute the budget and current account deficits to the high spending of successive Greek governments.[11]

Greece funded these twin deficits by borrowing in international capital markets, leaving it with a chronically high external debt (116% of GDP in 2009).[12] Both Greece's budget deficit and external debt level are well above those permitted by the rules governing the EU's Economic and Monetary Union (EMU). Specifically, the Treaty on European Union, commonly referred to as the Maastricht Treaty, calls for budget deficit ceilings of 3% of

GDP and external debt ceilings of 60% of GDP. Greece is not alone, however, in exceeding these limits. Of the 27 EU member states, 25 exceed these limits.[13]

Greece's reliance on external financing for funding budget and current account deficits left its economy highly vulnerable to shifts in investor confidence. Although the outbreak of the global financial crisis in fall 2008 led to a liquidity crisis for many countries, including several Central and Eastern European countries, the Greek government initially weathered the crisis relatively well and had been able to continue accessing new funds from international markets. However, the global recession resulting from the financial crisis put strain on many governments' budgets, including Greece's, as spending increased and tax revenues weakened. [14]

Outbreak of the Current Crisis

Since late 2009, investor confidence in the Greek government has been rattled. In October 2009, the new socialist government, led by Prime Minister George Papandreou, revised the estimate of the government budget deficit for 2009, nearly doubling the existing estimate of 6.7% of GDP to 12.7% of GDP.[15] This was shortly followed by rating downgrades of Greek bonds by the three major credit rating agencies. In late November 2009, questions about whether Dubai World, a state-controlled enterprise in Dubai, would default on its debt raised additional concerns about the possibility of a cascade of sovereign defaults for governments under the strain of the financial crisis. Countries with large external debts, like Greece, were of particular concern for investors. Allegations that Greek governments had falsified statistics and attempted to obscure debt levels through complex financial instruments also contributed to a drop in investor confidence.[16] Before the crisis, Greek 10-year bond yields were 10 to 40 basis points above German 10-year bonds. With the crisis, this spread increased to 400 basis points in January 2010, which was at the time a record high.[17] High bond spreads indicate declining investor confidence in the Greek economy.

Despite increasing nervousness surrounding Greece's economy, the Greek government was able to successfully sell €8 billion ($10.2 billion) in bonds at the end of January 2010, €5 billion ($6.4 billion) at the end of March 2010, and €1.56 billion ($1.99 billion) in mid-April 2010, albeit at high interest rates. However, Greece must borrow an additional €54 billion ($68.8 billion) to cover maturing debt and interest payments in 2010, and concerns began to develop about the government's ability to do so.[18]

At the end of March 2010, Eurozone member states pledged to provide financial assistance to Greece in concert with the IMF, if necessary, and if requested by Greece's government. Negotiations and discussions about the package continued and investor jitteriness spiked again in April 2010, when Eurostat, the EU's statistical agency, released its estimate of Greece's budget deficit. At 13.6% of GDP, Eurostat's estimate was almost a full percentage point higher than the previous estimate released by the Greek government in October 2009. This led to renewed questions about Greece's ability to repay its debts, with €8.5 billion ($10.8 billion) falling due on May 19, 2010. On April 23, 2010, the Greek government formally requested financial assistance from the IMF and other Eurozone countries. The European Commission, backed by Germany, requested that more details on Greece's proposed budget cuts for 2010, 2011, and 2012 be released before providing the financial assistance. In late April 2010, the spread between Greek and German 10-year bonds reached a record high of 650 basis points,[19] and one of the major credit rating agencies, Moody's, downgraded Greece's bond rating by one notch. On April 27, 2010, another ratings agency, Standard and Poor's, downgraded Greek bonds to "junk" status.

In meetings with members of the German Parliament (*Bundestag*), IMF Managing Director Dominique Strauss-Kahn reportedly raised the prospect of a three-year assistance package to Greece totaling €120 billion ($152 billion), substantially larger than initially reported in news reports. As negotiations among the IMF, Eurozone member states, and Greece continued, Greece agreed to additional austerity measures. On May 2, 2010, the Eurozone and IMF announced a three-year, €110 billion (about $145 billion) stabilization plan for Greece. Eurozone countries are to contribute €80 billion (about $105 billion) in bilateral loans, pending parliamentary approval in some countries. The IMF is to contribute a €30 billion (about $40 billion) loan at market-based interest rates. The agreement is considered historic, because it is the first IMF loan to a Eurozone country and the overall package is substantial relative to Greece's GDP (forecasted to be €229 billion [$291 billion] in 201 0).[20] In exchange for financial assistance, Greece submitted a three- year plan aimed at cutting its budget deficit from 13.6% of GDP in 2009 to below 3% of GDP in 2014. The Eurozone/IMF package was announced amidst Greek protests that at times started turning violent.

Despite the substantial size of the financial assistance package, the threat of Greece's crisis spreading to other Eurozone countries remained. Bond spreads for several other European countries spiked and the euro started to depreciate rapidly. In a bid to "save the euro," on May 9, 2010, European Union governments announced that they would make an additional €500 billion (about $636 billion) available to vulnerable European countries. The IMF may contribute up to an additional €220 billion (about $280 billion) to €250 billion (about $318 billion). Following the announcement, the market reacted positively, as bond spreads for several vulnerable European countries dropped and the euro began to strengthen.

Possible Causes of Greece's Crisis

Greece's current economic problems have been caused by a mix of domestic and international factors. Domestically, high government spending, structural rigidities, tax evasion, and corruption have all contributed to Greece's accumulation of debt over the past decade. Internationally, the adoption of the euro and lax enforcement of EU rules aimed at limiting the accumulation of debt are also believed to have contributed to Greece's current crisis.

Domestic Factors

High Government Spending and Weak Government Revenues

Between 2001 and 2007, Greece's GDP grew at an average annual rate of 4.3%, compared to a Eurozone average of 3.1%.[21] High economic growth rates were driven primarily by increases in private consumption (largely fueled by easier access to credit) and public investment financed by the EU and the central government. Over the past six years, however, while central government expenditures increased by 87%, revenues grew by only 31%, leading to budget deficits well above the EU's agreed-upon threshold of 3%.[22] Observers also identify a large and inefficient public administration, costly pension and healthcare systems, tax evasion, and a general "absence of the will to maintain fiscal discipline" as major factors behind Greece's deficit.[23]

According to the OECD, as of 2004, spending on public administration as a percentage of total public expenditure in Greece was higher than in any other OECD member, "with no evidence that the quantity or quality of the services are superior."[24] This trend has continued. Greek government expenditures in

2009 accounted for 50% of GDP, with 75% of (non-interest) public spending going to wages and social benefits.[25] Successive Greek governments have taken steps to modernize and consolidate the public administration. However, observers continue to cite overstaffing and poor productivity in the public sector as an impediment to improved economic performance. An aging Greek population—the percentage of Greeks aged over 64 is expected to rise from 19% in 2007 to 32% in 2060—could place additional burdens on public spending and what is widely considered one of Europe's most generous pension systems. According to the OECD, Greece's "replacement rate of 70%-80% of wages (plus any benefits from supplementary schemes) is high, and entitlement to a full pension requires only 35 years of contributions, compared to 40 in many other countries."[26] Absent reform, total Greek public pension payments are expected to increase from 11.5% of GDP in 2005 to 24% of GDP in 2050.

Weak revenue collection has also contributed to Greece's budget deficits. Many economists identify tax evasion and Greece's unrecorded economy as key factors behind the deficits. They argue that Greece must address these problems if it is to raise the revenues necessary to improve its fiscal position. Some studies have valued the informal economy in Greece at between 25%-30% of GDP.[27] Observers offer a variety of explanations for the prevalence of tax evasion in Greece, including high levels of taxation and a complex tax code, excessive regulation, and inefficiency in the public sector. Like his predecessor Constantine (Costas) Karamanlis, Prime Minister Papandreou has committed to cracking down on tax and social security contribution evasion. Observers note, however, that past Greek governments have had, at best, mixed success seeing through similar initiatives.

Structural Policies and Declining International Competitiveness

Greek industry is suffering from declining international competitiveness. Economists cite high relative wages and low productivity as a primary factor. According to one study, wages in Greece have increased at a 5% annual rate since the country adopted the euro, about double the average rate in the Eurozone as a whole. Over the same period, Greek exports to its major trading partners grew at 3.8% per year, only half the rate of those countries' imports from other trading partners.[28] Some observers argue that for Greece to boost the competitiveness of its industries and reduce its current account deficit, it needs to increase its productivity, significantly cut wages, and increase savings. As discussed below, the Papandreou government has begun to curb public sector wages and hopes to increase Greek exports through investment in areas where the country has a comparative advantage. In the past, tourism and the shipping industry have been the Greek economy's strongest sectors.

International Factors

Increased Access to Capital at Low Interest Rates

Greece's adoption of the euro as its national currency in 2001 is seen by some as a contributing factor in Greece's buildup of debt. With the currency bloc anchored by economic heavyweights Germany and France, and a common monetary policy conservatively managed by the ECB, investors have tended to view the reliability of euro member countries with a heightened degree of confidence. The perceptions of stability conferred by euro membership allowed Greece, as well as other Eurozone members, to borrow at a more favorable interest rate than would likely have been the case outside the EU, making it easier to finance the state budget and service existing debt. This benefit, however, may also have contributed to Greece's current debt problems: observers argue that access to artificially cheap credit allowed Greece to accumulate high levels of debt. Critics assert that if the market had discouraged excess borrowing by making debt financing more expensive, Greece would have been forced to come to terms earlier with the need for austerity and reform.

Issues with EU Rules Enforcement

The lack of enforcement of the Stability and Growth Pact is also seen as a contributing factor to Greece's high level of debt. In 1997, EU members adopted the Stability and Growth Pact, an agreement to enhance the surveillance and enforcement of the public finance rules set out in the 1992 Maastricht Treaty's "convergence criteria" for EMU. The rules call for government budget deficits not to exceed 3% of GDP and public debt not to exceed 60% of GDP. The 1997 Stability and Growth Pact clarified and sped up the excessive deficit procedure to be applied to member states that surpassed the deficit limit. If the member state is deemed to have insufficiently complied with the corrective measures recommended by the European Commission and the Council of the European Union during the excessive deficit procedure, the process may ultimately result in a fine of as much as 0.5% of GDP.[29]

Following the launch of the euro in 1999, an increasing number of member states found it hard to comply with the limits set by the Pact. Since 2003, more than 30 excessive deficit procedures have been undertaken, with the EU reprimanding member states and pressuring them to consolidate public finances, or at least promise to do so. The EU, however, has never imposed a financial sanction against any member state for violating the deficit limit. The lack of enforcement of the Stability and Growth Pact is thought to have limited the role the EU can play in discouraging countries, like Greece, from running up high levels of debt.

The European Commission initiated an excessive deficit procedure against Greece in 2004 when Greece reported an upward revision of its 2003 budget deficit figure to 3.2% of GDP. In its report, the Commission indicated that "the quality of public data is not satisfactory," noting that the EU's statistical office, Eurostat, had not certified or had unilaterally amended data provided by the National Statistical Service of Greece since 2000.[30] Subsequent statistical revisions between 2004 and 2007 revealed that Greece had violated the 3% limit in every year since 2000, with its deficit topping out at 7.9% of GDP in 2004. The Commission also noted that Greece's debt had been above 100% of GDP since before Greece joined the euro, and that the statistical revisions had pushed the debt number up as well. The EU closed the excessive deficit procedure in 2007, with the Commission pronouncing itself satisfied that Greece had taken sufficient measures, "mainly of a permanent nature," and that the country's deficit would be 2.6% of GDP in 2006 and 2.4% in 2007.

The Commission also concluded that "the Greek statistical authorities improved their procedures," leading to "an overall higher quality of data."[31] The Commission opened a new excessive deficit procedure in 2009 when Greece's 2007 deficit was reported at 3.5% of GDP, and that procedure is ongoing in the context of the current situation.[32] This points to a broader problem of a monetary union without a fiscal union, as discussed below in "European Integration."

Addressing Greece's Crisis: Progress to Date

The Greek government faces government budget and current account deficits that it can no longer finance by borrowing from international capital markets. Some caution that Greece is at risk of defaulting on its debt obligations. To address this crisis, the government is pursuing a mix of fiscal austerity (government spending cuts and tax increases) and structural reforms to improve the competitiveness of the economy. Financial assistance from the other Eurozone member states and the IMF is allowing the adjustment to take place over a longer time period. Some economists have concern that despite the government's reforms and the financial assistance from other Eurozone member states and the IMF, the Greek government may still default on or restructure its debt and/or leave the Eurozone. Amidst concerns that Greece's crisis spreading throughout the Eurozone, the EU has announced it will make substantial resources available to vulnerable European countries.

Greek Domestic Policy Responses

Fiscal Austerity

Since taking office in October 2009, the Papandreou government has unveiled four separate packages of fiscal austerity measures aimed at bringing Greece's government deficit down from an estimated 13.6% of GDP in 2009 to below 3% by 2014.[33] The government had hoped that three rounds of spending cuts and tax increases announced between January 2010 and March 2010 would restore enough investor confidence in the Greek economy to eliminate the need for outside financial assistance. Financial markets did not react as hoped, and in late April 2010, the Greek government requested assistance from the IMF and EU. The IMF and EU, in turn, called on Athens to implement additional austerity measures. In an emotional and contentious vote, the Greek parliament approved the latest measures on May 6, 2010.

The Papandreou government's three-year fiscal consolidation plan is centered on deep cuts to public spending and enhanced revenue growth through tax increases and a crack-down on tax and social security contribution evasion. On the spending side, most of the cuts focus on the civil service. They include a reduction or freeze on all civil service pensions, wages, and bonuses and a civil servant hiring freeze in 2010 with a 5:1 retirement/recruitment ratio for new public sector hires from 2011. On the revenue side, the government has raised the average value-added tax rate from 19% to 23% and increased taxes on fuel, tobacco, liquor, and luxury products, among other things.[34] The government hopes to raise revenues equivalent to 1.8% of GDP through strengthened tax collection and higher contribution requirements for tax evaders.

Eurozone member states have welcomed the Papandreou government's plans for fiscal consolidation. Some observers express concern, however, that the mix of tax increases and sharp spending cuts could lead to higher unemployment and deepen an ongoing recession in the country. The policy solutions to two of the major economic issues facing the Greek government—cutting large government budget deficits (which requires contractionary fiscal policies to address) and stimulating the economy during cyclical economic downturn (which requires expansionary fiscal policies)—are at odds with each other. Some question, then, how long the government will be able to count on public support for the contractionary measures in the face of a sharp recession.[35]

Structural Reforms

Prime Minister Papandreou has repeatedly emphasized the need for longer-term structural reforms to the Greek economy. To this end, he has proposed wide-ranging reforms to the pension and health care systems and to Greece's public administration. His government has also announced measures to boost Greek economic competitiveness by enhancing employment and economic growth, fostering increased private sector development, and supporting research, technology, and innovation.

As mentioned above, the Greek pension system, considered one of the most generous in Europe, has long been a target of advocates of Greek economic reform. The Papandreou government has pledged both to reform pension institutions and to crack down on social security contribution evasion. The government has said it will raise the average retirement age from 61 to 63 (the statutory retirement age in Greece is 65) and begin calculating pensions on the basis of lifetime contributions as opposed to the last five years of earnings, as is now the case with some civil service pension schemes.[36] Prime Minister Papandreou has announced a similar effort to tighten public regulation and strengthen accountability in what is widely considered an inefficient Greek health care system. His government also hopes to restructure Greece's public administration. This includes consolidating local governance structures by reducing the levels of local administrative authorities from five to three, reducing the number of Greek municipalities from 1,034 to 370, and reducing the legal public entities formed by local authorities from 6,000 to 2,000.

Challenges and Prospects

Some economists express concern that Greece's relatively drastic contractionary fiscal policies could prolong an ongoing recession in the country. GDP contracted by 2% in 2009 and is forecasted to contract by anywhere from 3% to 5% in 2010 and by 0.5% to 1.6% in 2011.[37] Registered unemployment reached 10.6% in November 2009, the highest level since March 2005, and is expected to increase in 2010 and 2011. As of October 2009, 27.5% of young people (aged 15-24) in Greece were unemployed.[38]

The Papandreou government hopes to counter these trends by attracting new foreign investment in Greece and by boosting exports of goods and services. In addition to advancing institutional reforms designed to more efficiently disburse Greek and EU investment and development funds, it intends to target sectors where it believes Greece has strong comparative advantages for trade and investment. These include its geographic location, particularly as a potential hub for regional trade and investment in energy and transportation networks; the renewable energy sector; and already strong global shipping and tourism sectors. Most agree, however, that the challenges to building sustainable economic growth are considerable. Greek exports dropped by close to 18% in 2009, and Greek businesses have become increasingly uncompetitive in domestic and international markets.[39]

Perhaps the most substantial challenge for the Greek government could be maintaining public and political support for its austerity and economic reform program. Papandreou's Panhellenic Socialist Movement (PASOK) came to office in October 2009 on a platform of "social protection" promising to boost wages, improve support for the poor, and promote redistribution of income. The policies his government has since pursued to cut the budget deficit have required retreating from most of these campaign pledges and could prove politically difficult to see through. Thousands of public sector workers and their supporters have taken to the streets to protest the austerity measures and more protests are scheduled. The protests turned deadly on May 5, 2010, when three people were killed during an attack on an Athens bank. Despite growing public opposition to his austerity program, Papandreou has secured parliamentary support of the measures. A majority of Greeks appear to recognize the need for fiscal consolidation and see PASOK as the most credible political party to see this through. Observers emphasize, however, that support for Papandreou could be contingent on whether his government's austerity measures are seen as fair and just. In this regard, the focus on reforming what is widely viewed as a corrupt and bloated public sector could benefit Papandreou.

Greece's largest opposition party, the center-right New Democracy (ND) unseated by PASOK in the 2009 elections, supported the first three rounds of fiscal consolidation measures taken by the Papandreou government, but opposed the May 6, 2010, measures. ND criticized Papandreou's decision to call for IMF assistance, with ND party leader Antonis Samaras predicting that the "IMF is going to force new measures upon [Greece] that neither [the Greek] economy nor [Greek] society will be able to bear."[40] Long-time observers of Greece point out that the reform record of past Greek governments dating back to the 1980s is mixed at best. It remains to be seen whether the Papandreou government will maintain the public support and political will to see through its wide range of reform proposals.

Eurozone/IMF Financial Assistance to Greece

On May 2, 2010, Eurozone finance ministers and the IMF agreed on a three-year program of loans to Greece totaling €110 billion (about $145 billion): €80 billion (about $105 billion) from Eurozone member states and €30 billion (about $40 billion) from the IMF. The package could reportedly provide €30 billion (about $40 billion) from the Eurozone and €10 billion (about $13 billion) from the IMF in 2010 to help ensure that Greece meets its immediate payment obligations.[41] The breakdown of the financial assistance package for Greece is shown in **Figure 1** and discussed in greater detail below.

Eurozone Member States

Details on Eurozone Member State Assistance to Greece

Over the course of March and April 2010, Eurozone leaders incrementally formulated a mechanism for providing financial assistance to Greece. After considerable negotiation, leaders agreed that the Eurozone countries would provide bilateral loans, at a market-based interest rate (approximately 5%, which is lower than what Greece had paid in recent bond sales), if supplemented by additional loans from the IMF and if the Greek government implemented substantial austerity measures over the next three years. On April 23, 2010, the Greek government formally requested the activation of this mechanism and the final package was announced the following week.

Of the Eurozone member states, Germany is reportedly providing the largest loan, expected to be €22.4 billion (about $29 billion) over the three-year period, followed by France, which is expected to loan Greece €16.8 billion (about $22 billion).[42] With payment deadlines on Greek bonds looming, European leaders are aiming to execute the loan arrangements quickly. Due to different legal requirements among Eurozone countries—final approval requires a parliamentary vote in some countries—the loans will likely not all be available at the same time. Advocates of quick implementation overcame a major hurdle, however, when the German parliament approved German participation in the plan on May 7, 2010.

Debates over Eurozone Member State Involvement

Prior to the decision to loan Greece money, the debate about potential Eurozone assistance was contentious. Some observers argued that there are compelling reasons for the other Eurozone countries to intervene, asserting that the financial stability of the Eurozone, and possibly even the future of the euro, might be at stake. Severe instability in the Greek economy had already started to have wider consequences—the crisis contributed to a weakening of the euro and raised concerns that it could spread across European bond markets and draw in countries such as Spain, Portugal, Italy, and Ireland. Some observers note that the Greek crisis grew worse as Eurozone leaders contemplated a response—critics charge that quicker action may have stemmed the crisis at an earlier stage. There is also a significant political element to the debate. Monetary union is seen by many proponents of a strong EU as a crowning achievement of European integration. Some observers, therefore, assert that the EU must maintain solidarity and that the countries of the Eurozone cannot not allow Greece to default, much less abandon the euro.

At the same time, there was also great reluctance to provide assistance to Greece. Many Eurozone countries are themselves experiencing financial difficulties, and many are exasperated by the idea of rescuing a country that, in their perspective, has not exercised budget discipline, has failed to modernize its economy, and has allegedly falsified past financial statistics. In addition, many strongly wish to avoid setting a precedent by "bailing out" a country that has not managed its finances well. Some observers argued that allowing Greece to default could be preferable to a Eurozone rescue package, and some have advocated devising a mechanism to remove countries from the Eurozone that do not meet the requirements. Others have argued that the Eurozone loans are illegal under EU treaties or national laws. Germany, the Eurozone's largest economy and arguably its most influential national voice on economic policy, has been among the most skeptical member states. Polls show that a large majority of Germans are strongly against providing financial assistance to Greece, and German Chancellor Angela Merkel repeatedly put a brake on discussions about formulating a rescue package before ultimately assenting.

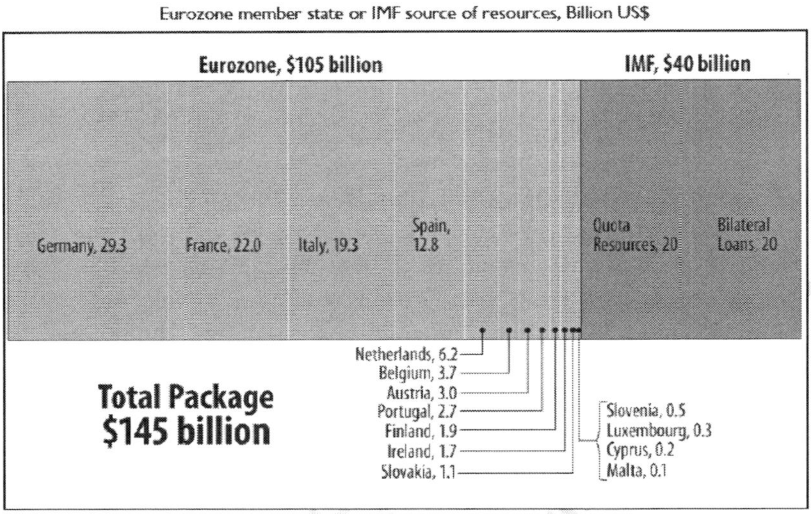

Source: Graphic prepared by CRS using data from Jan Strupczewski, "Factbox - Progress Towards Approving Emergency Loans to Greece," *Reuters*, May 6, 2010. IMF data from IMF, "Frequently Asked Questions: Greece," May 11, 2010, *http://www.imf.org /external/np/exr/faq/greecefaqs.htm#q23.*

Notes: Eurozone member state commitments are bilateral loans, and some commitments are subject to parliamentary approval. IMF quota resources and bilateral loans fund a Stand-By Arrangement (SBA) loan for Greece. Conversion to dollars from euros using exchange rate of €1 = $1.31 8.

Figure 1. Eurozone/IMF Financial Assistance Package for Greece.

IMF

Details on IMF Assistance to Greece

Approximately one-third of the Eurozone and IMF financial package for Greece is from IMF resources. The IMF assistance to Greece is a three-year, $40 billion loan made at market-based interest rates. Specifically, it is a three-year Stand-By Arrangement (SBA), which is the IMF's standard loan vehicle for addressing balance-of-payments difficulties. The IMF does not disburse the full amount of its loans to governments at once. Instead, the IMF will divide the loan into tranches (French for "slice") and will only disburse the next tranche after verifying that the specified economic policy reforms have been met. Urging policy reforms in this way ensures that the loans will be repaid to the IMF,[43] and that the required economic reforms are implemented.

Greece's loan from the Fund is unusual for two reasons. First, the IMF does not generally lend to developed countries and has never lent to a Eurozone member state since the euro was introduced in 1999 as an accounting currency and 2002 as physical currency in circulation. Second, it is unusual for its relative magnitude. The IMF has general limits on the amount it will lend to a country either through a SBA or Extended Fund Facility (EFF), which is similar to a SBA but for countries facing longer-term balance-of-payments problems. The IMF's guidelines for limits on the size of loans for SBAs and EFFs are 200% of a member's quota annually and 600% of a member's quota cumulatively.[44] IMF quotas are the financial commitment that IMF members make upon joining the Fund and are broadly based on the IMF member's relative size in the world economy. In "exceptional" situations, the IMF reserves the right to lend in excess of these limits, and has done so in the past. The IMF 's loan to Greece is indeed exceptional access at 3,200% of Greece's IMF quota and is the largest access of IMF quota resources granted to an IMF member country.[45]

The IMF is expected to finance half of Greece's loan ($20 billion) using IMF quota resources. Although the United States has contributed 17% of IMF quota resources, it is unclear what portion of the IMF loan for Greece that is financed by quota resources will be funded by the U.S. quotas. The IMF does not disclose country contributions to individual transactions with the Fund. In deciding which quota resources to use, the IMF aims to provide a balanced position for all members.

The other half ($20 billion) of the IMF loan is expected to be financed by bilateral loans that have been committed to the IMF as part of an overall effort to increase IMF resources. None of this portion is coming from the United States. In 2009, the United States did agree to extend a line of credit worth $100 billion as part of expanding the IMF's New Arrangements to Borrow (NAB). However, the expanded NAB is not yet operational, so this $100 billion line of credit from the United States cannot be tapped for Greece's package.

Debates over IMF Involvement

At the onset of the Greek crisis, many EU officials were insistent that the Eurozone take ownership of the issue. Analysts asserted that it was important for the Eurozone to demonstrate its strength and credibility by taking care of its own problems. The prospect of "outside" intervention from the IMF was viewed by many as a potential "humiliation" for the Eurozone, with officials at the ECB, among others, strongly opposed.[46] In late March, however, the debate in Europe appeared to shift, with the door slowly opening for possible IMF involvement as a number of member states came to favor a twin-track approach combining Eurozone and IMF financial assistance.

In the end, IMF involvement was reportedly a key condition of German Chancellor Merkel's willingness to provide financial assistance to Greece. Some argue that the policy reforms (conditionality) attached to an IMF loan would lend additional impetus to reform and provide both the Greek government and the EU with an outside scapegoat for pushing through politically unpopular reforms. The EU would also make policy reforms a condition of loans, but the IMF is seen as more independent than the EU and has more experience in resolving debt crises than the EU.[4]

Are the Domestic Reforms and Eurozone/IMF Package for Greece Enough?

Some economists fear that Greece's fiscal austerity plan, which entails cutting budget deficits by 9% of GDP in four years, is too ambitious and will be politically difficult to implement.[48] As a result, some economists suggest that the Greek government could still default on or, considered more plausible, restructure its debt. In fact, some observers regret that debt restructuring was not included in the IMF package in order to provide a more orderly debt workout.[49] Restructuring would also push some of costs of the crisis onto private banks that, it is argued, engaged in "reckless lending" to Greece. [50] However, a default or debt restructuring could accelerate the contagion of the crisis to other Eurozone countries, as well as hinder Greece's ability to regain access to capital markets. In addition, even if Greece's government stopped servicing its debt, it would still need substantial fiscal austerity measures to address the government deficit unrelated to debt payments.

This has led some economists to argue that Greek fiscal austerity should be offset by more accommodating monetary policy by the ECB. This seems unlikely in light of recent reported comments by the President of the ECB, Jean-Claude Trichet, on the ECB's commitment to price stability.[51]

As a result, some economists have suggested that Greece should or may leave the Eurozone.[52] This would likely require abandoning the euro, issuing a national currency, and allowing that currency to depreciate against the euro. The Greek government would also probably have to put restrictions on bank withdrawals to prevent a run on the banks during the transition from the euro to a national currency. It is thought that a new national currency depreciated against the euro would spur export-led growth in Greece and offset the contractionary effects of austerity. Since Greece's debt is denominated in euros, however, leaving the Eurozone in favor of a depreciated national currency would raise the value of Greece's debt in terms of national currency and put pressure on other vulnerable European countries. Additionally, some argue that a Greek departure from the Eurozone would be economically catastrophic, creating the "mother of all financial crises,"[53] and have serious ramifications for political relations among the European states and future European integration.

Broader EU Stabilization Package

EU Member States

Despite the enactment of the Eurozone-IMF assistance package for Greece, investor concerns about the sustainability of Eurozone debt deepened during the first week of May 2010. Driven down by such fears, global stock markets plunged sharply on May 6, 2010, and the euro fell to a 15-month low against the dollar. Seeking to head off the possibility of contagion to countries such as Portugal and Spain, EU finance ministers agreed to a broader €500 billion (about $686 billion) "European Financial Stabilization Mechanism" on May 9, 2010. Some analysts assert that such a bold, large-scale move had become an urgent imperative for the EU in order to break the momentum of a gathering European financial crisis. Investors reacted positively to the announcement of the new agreement, with global stock markets rebounding on May 10, 2010, to re-gain the sharp losses of the week before.

The bulk of the European Financial Stabilization Mechanism package consists of a "Special Purpose Vehicle" under which Eurozone countries could make available bilateral loans and government-backed loan guarantees totaling up to €440 billion (about $560 billion) to stabilize the euro area. The agreement, which expires after three years, requires parliamentary ratification in some Eurozone countries. The mechanism additionally allows the European Commission to raise money on capital markets and loan up to €60 billion (about $76 billion) to Eurozone states. Previously, such a procedure could only be applied to non-Eurozone members of the EU, and was used after the global financial crisis to improve the balance-of-payments situations of Latvia, Hungary, and Romania. Lastly, the ECB may take on a more significant new role: if necessary to increase market confidence, the ECB can now buy member state bonds, an activity in which it has not previously engaged.

IMF

The European Financial Stabilization Mechanism was announced with the IMF contributing up to an additional €220 billion to €250 billion (about $280 billion to $318 billion). This is in line with the Greece package, where the Eurozone states contributed roughly 2/3 and the IMF 1/3. IMF Managing Director John Lipsky reportedly later clarified the news reports about the IMF contribution to the European Financial Stabilization Mechanism, saying that these pledges were "illustrative" of the support that the IMF could provide.[54] Reportedly, Lipsky reiterated that the IMF only provides loans to countries that have requested IMF assistance and that Greece is the only Eurozone country to date that has requested IMF assistance.

IMPLICATIONS OF GREECE'S CRISIS

Contagion and Eurozone Debt Concerns

Prior to the agreement on the European Financial Stabilization Mechanism, growing spreads on Portuguese and Spanish bonds, coupled with the late April 2010 downgrades of those countries' credit ratings, raised renewed concerns about the possibility of contagion within the Eurozone. Concerns about a spillover of Greece's crisis to its neighbors are rooted in memories of the Asian financial crisis in 1997-1998, where it is believed that investor herding behavior contributed to the spread of the crisis throughout the region.[55]

As investors become increasingly nervous about the sustainability of some countries' debt, the higher interest rates demanded for new bonds make it in turn more difficult for those countries to borrow and to service their existing debt. Should a loss of market confidence take hold and spread, investors could rush to sell off the bonds they hold and decline to buy new bonds that countries seek to auction: a cascade of sovereign debt crises could result. While investor confidence is based primarily on conditions within each country, confidence in this case had also been affected by the gradual reaction to the Greek crisis, as some observers came to doubt the willingness and ability of the Eurozone and the IMF to tackle another crisis in Europe.

The European Financial Stabilization Mechanism appears to have successfully reassured the markets and diminished the likelihood of a Eurozone contagion scenario for the time being. Nevertheless, some observers assert that the mechanism does not solve the root causes of the problem, and that numerous European countries will still need to take difficult steps to increase their industrial competitiveness and improve the state of their public finances. Portugal and Spain had been thought by many to be the leading candidates for the next potential crisis, and Italy and Ireland have been frequently mentioned as well. Although these countries all borrowed heavily during the credit bubble that preceded the global financial crisis, the economic circumstances and challenges differ in each one. In noting the size of the Italian and Spanish economies compared to the much smaller Greek, Irish, and Portuguese economies, observers caution that a financial crisis affecting one of the larger countries could pose a problem of a much higher magnitude.

Complex Financial Instruments and Financial Regulation

Through the crisis, it has been reported that Greek governments, underwritten by prominent financial institutions including Goldman Sachs, used complex financial instruments to conceal the true level of Greece's debt.[56] For example, the government of Papandreou's predecessor, Costas Karamanlis, is alleged to have exchanged future revenues from Greece's highways, airports, and lotteries for up-front cash payments from investors. Likewise, it is reported that the Greek government borrowed billions by trading currencies at favorable exchange rates. Because these transactions were technically considered currency swaps, not loans, they did not need to be reported by the Greek government under EU accounting rules. The Federal Reserve is currently investigating the role that Goldman Sachs and other U.S. financial institutions played in the buildup of Greece's debt.[57]

The role of complex financial instruments in Greece's debt crisis has exposed some tensions between the United States and the EU over financial regulation. Some European leaders have called for tighter financial regulation, including a prohibition on derivatives that are believed to have helped create Greece's debt crisis. Financial regulatory reform before Congress would regulate, but not ban, derivatives. In a mid-March 2010 visit to Washington, DC, Prime Minister Papandreou vocally criticized "unprincipled speculators" for "making billions every day by betting on a Greek default."[58]

European Integration

Greece's debt crisis has also launched a number of broader debates about the EU's monetary union. Since the introduction of the euro in 1999, skeptics have pointed to a mismatch between the EU's advanced economic and monetary union and an incomplete political union. Even within the economic areas where the EU is more tightly integrated, the Eurozone has a single monetary policy but 16 separate (if loosely coordinated) national fiscal policies. Critics argue that this arrangement is prone to problems and imbalances that threaten the viability of having a common currency. Others assert that the Greek crisis points to the need for stronger EU economic governance, at the very least in the form of a tighter and more enforceable Stability and Growth Pact. Going further, some proponents of deeper integration would like to use the crisis to launch a discussion about moving towards a more integrated EU-wide fiscal policy.

Additionally, some officials and analysts have proposed that the EU create a new European Monetary Fund (EMF) that would allow it to respond more smoothly to financial crises within individual member states in the future, operating much like the IMF but on a regional, rather than global, basis. There is some discussion that this would require a new governing treaty for the EU, which may be politically difficult to pass. Following the Asian financial crisis in 1997-1998, similar proposals for creating an institution like the IMF, but operating specifically within the region, were discussed but no such institution was created.

Finally, Greece's crisis has brought to light imbalances within the Eurozone. Some Northern European countries, such as Germany, have relied on exports for economic growth and pursued policies that aim to promote such export-led growth, such as wage moderation to keep the costs of production low and make exports competitive. Combined with conservative fiscal policies that promote high levels of savings, these countries have run large current account surpluses. In contrast, some Southern European countries, like Greece, have had higher levels of wage growth and more expansionary fiscal policies, leading to less competitive exports and lower levels of savings. These countries have run large current account deficits and borrowed to finance these deficits.

Some argue that the Southern European countries now need to reduce their debt and increase savings, which translates to running current account surpluses.[59] Hopes for export-led growth may be difficult to realize, however, in the face of the global economic recession. Greece's reliance on tourism, which is highly affected by economic conditions (consumer spending on luxury items) and shipping, which is also affected by economic conditions (increased trade; low energy costs), raises real questions about trade providing much of a boost to the economy. Additionally, observers note that it is unclear whether the Northern European countries such as Germany are willing to take steps in their own domestic economies to reduce their levels of savings, curb exports, cut their current account surpluses, and promote this rebalancing within the Eurozone.[60] How imbalances will be resolved within the Eurozone may be an important component of debates about EU integration in the future.

U.S. Economy

In addition to shaping debates over regulatory reform, both between the United States and the EU as well as within the G-20 more broadly,[61] Greece's debt crisis could have at least five major implications for the United States. First is the exchange rate. Many expect that if investors lose confidence in the future of the Eurozone, and more current account adjustment is required for the Eurozone as a whole, the value of the euro will weaken.[62] Already, the euro has depreciated in recent months against the U.S. dollar (**Figure 2**), falling by more than 15% between December 12, 2009 and May 7, 2010, (from 1.51 $/€ to 1.27 $/€). A weaker euro would likely lower U.S. exports to the Eurozone and increase U.S. imports from the Eurozone, widening the U.S. trade deficit.[63] On the other hand, it will make purchases and U.S. investments in Eurozone countries cheaper in dollar terms.

Second, the United States has a large financial stake in the EU. The EU as a whole is the United States's biggest trading partner and hundreds of billions of dollars flow between the EU and the United States each year.[64] Widespread financial instability in the EU could impact trade and growth in the region, which in turn could impact the U.S. economy. On the other hand, instability in the EU may make the United States more attractive to investors and encourage capital flows to the United States. However, if the crisis is contained to Greece, the effects on the United States would be smaller than instability throughout the EU as a whole.

Third, a Greek default could have implications for U.S. commercial interests. Although most of Greece's debt is held by Europeans, $16.6 billion of Greece's debt obligations are owed to creditors within the United States.[65]

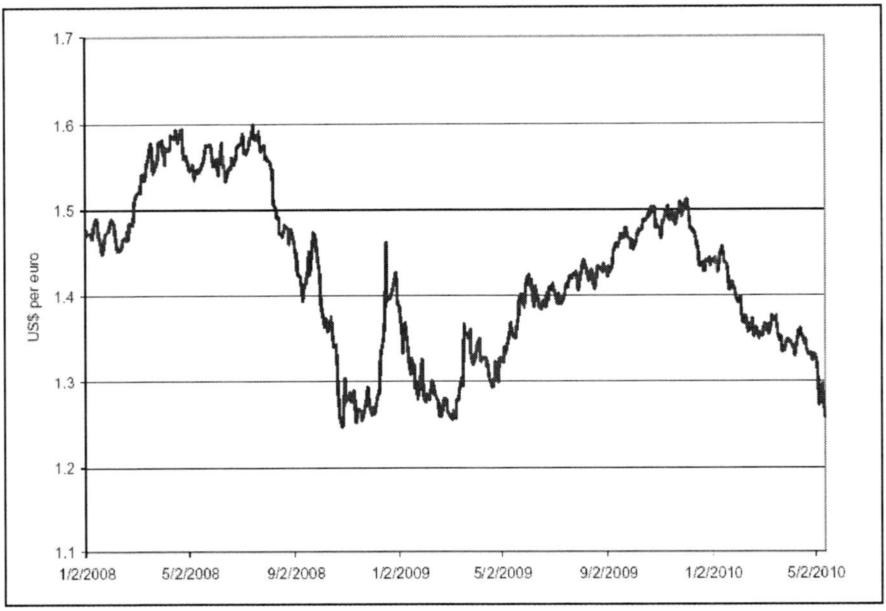

Source: European Central Bank (ECB).

Figure 2. US$/Euro Exchange Rate, January 2008 – May 2010.

Although not an insignificant amount of money, the relative size of U.S. creditor exposure to Greek bonds however is likely too small to create significant effects on the U.S. economy overall if Greece were to default.

Fourth, the global recession has worsened the government budget position of a large number of countries. Some argue that credit markets may have awakened to the magnitude of the debt problem due to the large number of countries that are involved and the extent of the budget deficits. For example, some have argued that there are strong similarities between Greece's financial situation and the financial situation in the United States.[66] Like Greece, it is argued, the United States has been reliant on foreign investors to fund a large budget deficit, resulting in rising levels of external debt and vulnerability to a sudden reversal in investor confidence. Others point out that the United States, unlike Greece, has a floating exchange rate and its currency is an international reserve currency, which alleviates many of the pressures associated with rising debt levels.

Fifth, debates over imbalances between current account deficit and current account surplus countries within the Eurozone are similar to the debates about imbalances between the United States and China. These debates reiterate how the economic policies of one country can affect other countries and the need for international economic cooperation and coordination to achieve international financial stability.

APPENDIX A. TIMELINE OF EVENTS SINCE APRIL 22, 2010

- **4/22/10** –Eurostat, the EU's statistical agency, announces its estimate of Greek government budget deficit for 2009: 13.6% of GDP. This is almost a full percentage point higher than 12.7% of GDP reported by Greek government in January 2010, and more than double the 6.7% of GDP reported by the previous Greek government before October 2009.
- **4/22/10** – Moody's downgrades Greek bonds one notch and places Greece on a negative outlook. Greek bond spreads widen. Yields on Greek 10-year bonds rise to 8.7%, compared to Germany's 10-year bonds at 3.04%.[67]
- **4/23/10** – The Greek government requests to draw on €45 billion (about $60 billion) in emergency financial assistance previously agreed by Eurozone members and the IMF: €30 billion (about $40 billion) from Eurozone member states and €15 billion (about $20 billion) from the IMF.
- **4/27/10** – Ratings agency Standard and Poor's downgrades Greek sovereign debt to "junk" status and downgrades Portuguese sovereign debt by two notches.
- **4/28/10** – Standard and Poor's downgrades Spanish sovereign bonds one notch.
- **4/28/10** – In meetings with Members of the German Parliament (*Bundestag*), IMF Managing Director Dominique Strauss-Kahn reportedly raises the prospect of a three-year assistance package to Greece totaling €120 billion (about $160 billion).
- **4/28/10** - Following the downgrade of its sovereign bonds, the Portuguese government reportedly announces it will immediately implement austerity measures initially planned for 2011 in an effort to regain investor confidence.
- **4/29/10** – Greece reportedly agrees to the outline of a €25.6 billion (about $32 billion) austerity package, including a three-year wage

freeze for public sector workers, in return for a multibillion-euro loan from the Eurozone and the IMF.

- **5/01/10** – Ongoing Greek protests against government austerity measures turn violent at times.
- **5/02/10** – The Eurozone and IMF announce a three-year, €110 billion (about $145 billion) stabilization plan for Greece. Eurozone countries are to contribute €80 billion (about $105 billion) in bilateral loans and the IMF is to provide €30 billion (about $40 billion) through a Stand-By Arrangement (SBA), the IMF's standard lending instrument. Greece's nominal GDP for 2010 is forecasted to be €229 billion (about $312 billion).[68] In exchange for financial assistance, Greece agrees to austerity measures worth 13% of national income over the next four years. Financial assistance cannot be disbursed until parliamentary approval is secured in the necessary countries (including Germany) and the IMF Executive Board approves the IMF loan.
- **5/03/10** – The European Central Bank (ECB) suspends the minimum credit rating required for Greek bonds used in ECB liquidity-providing operations. This policy change aims to sustain liquidity in the European banking sector.
- **5/05/10** – Three Greek bankers are killed in anti-reform riots.
- **5/06/10** – The Greek parliament passes austerity measures necessary for Eurozone and IMF financial assistance by a vote of 171 to 121.[69]
- **5/06/10** – Dow Jones drops nearly 1,000 points in less than half an hour. Initially, observers suspect contagion from Greece's debt crisis. Subsequent reports suggest that other factors were at play. The Dow Jones recovered to a loss of 347 points at the close.
- **5/07/10** – German, French, and Dutch parliaments approve financial assistance to Greece.
- **5/09/10** – The IMF Executive Board approves the loan to Greece.
- **5/09/10** –EU leaders announce that €500 billion (about $636 billion) will be available for vulnerable European countries, with the IMF ready to provide an additional €220 billion (about S280 billion) to €250 billion (about $318 billion). This assumes the same division as with the Greek package (2/3 from Eurozone, 1/3 from IMF). The IMF only provides financial assistance to countries that IMF only provides financial assistance, and Greece is the only Eurozone country that has requested assistance to date. The ECB also announced it would buy member state bonds, a change from previous policy.

- **5/09/10** – The U.S. Federal Reserve announces it will reopen currency swap lines with other major central banks, including the ECB, to help ease economic pressure.
- **5/10/10** – Markets react favorably to announcement of EU financial assistance package; bond spreads of vulnerable European countries fall and euro begins to strengthen.
- **5/19/10** – Greek debt worth €8.5 billion (about $10.8 billion) is scheduled to fall due.

APPENDIX B. ECONOMIC INDICATORS FOR SELECTED EUROZONE COUNTRIES AND THE UNITED STATES

Country	2005	2006	2007	2008	2009	2010	2011
Government budget, % of GDP							
Greece	-5.3	-3.2	-4.0	-7.8	-13.0[a]	-9.4	-6.0
Portugal	-6.0	-3.9	-2.7	-2.8	-9.4	-8.5	-7.1
Spain	1.0	2.0	1.9	-4.1	-11.4	-11.5	-9.5
Italy	-4.2	-3.3	-1.5	-2.7	-5.3	-5.3	-5.1
Ireland	1.7	3.0	0.2	-7.2	-12.0	-12.5	-9.8
Germany	-3.3	-1.6	0.2	0.0	-3.1	-5.6	-5.2
France	-3.0	-2.3	-2.7	-3.3	-7.5	-8.4	-7.9
Netherlands	-0.3	0.5	0.2	0.7	-5.3	-6.2	-5.1
United Kingdom	-3.3	-2.6	-2.6	-4.9	-11.4	-12.8	-10.9
United States	-2.6	-1.9	-1.2	-3.1	-9.9	-11.1	-10.8
Public debt, % of GDP							
Greece	114.5	107.9	103.9	102.6	116.3	130.1	136.2
Portugal	63.6	64.7	63.6	66.3	76.9	85.0	91.0
Spain	43.0	39.6	36.2	39.7	55.2	67.4	77.0
Italy	105.8	106.4	103.4	106.1	115.2	119.6	120.3
Ireland	27.2	24.9	24.2	44.0	62.2	76.6	87.6
Germany	68.1	67.6	64.9	66.0	72.0	77.1	80.1
France	66.4	63.6	63.8	67.5	77.5	84.4	89.8
Netherlands	51.8	47.4	45.5	58.2	63.1	67.8	71.2
United Kingdom	42.2	43.2	44.2	52.0	68.1	78.1	84.7
United States	36.9	36.5	36.2	37.5	47.3	54.5	64.5

Appendix B (Continued)

Current Account, % of GDP							
Greece	-7.5	-11.3	-14.4	-14.6	-11.2	-9.7	-8.1
Portugal	-9.5	-10.0	-9.4	-12.1	-10.1	-9.0	-10.2
Spain	-7.4	-9.0	-10.0	-9.6	-5.1	-5.3	-5.1
Italy	-1.7	-2.6	-2.4	-3.4	-3.4	-2.8	-2.7
Ireland	-3.5	-3.6	-5.3	-5.2	-2.9	0.4	-0.1
Germany	5.1	6.5	7.6	6.7	4.8	5.5	5.6
France	-0.4	-0.5	-1.0	-2.3	-1.5	-1.9	-1.8
Netherlands	7.3	9.3	8.7	4.8	5.2	5.0	5.3
United Kingdom	-2.6	-3.3	-2.7	-1.5	-1.3	-1.7	-1.6
United States	-5.9	-6.0	-5.2	-4.9	-2.9	-3.3	-3.4
GDP, Billion US$b							
Greece	243	264	310	352	331	325	321
Portugal	186	195	223	245	228	226	228
Spain	1,132	1,236	1,443	1,602	1,464	1,425	1,433
Italy	1,781	1,865	2,119	2,307	2,118	2,121	2,159
Ireland	202	222	260	268	228	216	222
Germany	2,793	2,920	3,328	3,673	3,353	3,333	3,385
France	2,148	2,270	2,598	2,867	2,676	2,669	2,723
Netherlands	640	678	779	877	795	797	804
United Kingdom	2,283	2,443	2,800	2,684	2,184	2,223	2,297
United States	12,638	13,399	14,078	14,441	14,256	14,800	15,397

Source: Data on government budgets (%of GDP) and public debt (% of GDP) is from Economist Intelligence Unit (EIU) Country Reports, April 2010. Data on current accounts (% of GDP) and GDP is from the IMF's World Economic Outlook Database, April 2010.

Notes: EIU data for 2010 and 2011 are forecasts. World Economic Outlook forecasts start in 2008 or 2009 depending on the country and indicator.

a. Eurostat announced at the end of April 2010 that their estimate of Greece's fiscal deficit for 2009 to be 13.6% of GDP.

b. Net public debt for Portugal, France, the United Kingdom, and the United States.

ACKNOWLEDGMENTS

Amber Wilhelm, Graphics Specialist, prepared Figure 1.

End Notes

[1] Jon Hilsenrath, "Q&A: Carmen Reinhart on Greece, U.S. Debt and Other 'Scary Scenarios'," *Wall Street Journal*, February 5, 2010.

[2] Carmen Reinhart, "The Economic and Fiscal Consequences of Financial Crises," VoxEU, January 26, 2009.

[3] For more on the global financial crisis, see CRS Report RL34742, *The Global Financial Crisis: Analysis and Policy Implications*, coordinated by Dick K. Nanto.

[4] For the Greek financial assistance package and the broader Eurozone financial assistance package, the exchange rate at the time the package was announced is used. Otherwise in the report, the exchange rate used is the exchange rate as of May 6, 2010: €1 = $1.2727. Source: European Central Bank, *http://www.ecb.int/stats/exchange/eurofxref/ html/eur ofxref-graph*. However, as noted later in the report, currency swings are underway, and dollar conversions of data denominated in euros should be approached as estimates.

[5] Provisional data for end-2009 Q4. Bank for International Settlements (BIS), "Consolidated International Claims of BIS Reporting Banks," Table 9B: Consolidated Foreign Claims of Reporting Banks - Immediate Borrower Basis, http://www.bis.org/statistics

[6] Steven Erlanger, Katrin Bennhold, and David E. Sanger, "Debt Aid Package for Europe Took Nudge from Washington," *New York Times*, May 10, 2010.

[7] Ibid.

[8] Kerin Hope, James Politi, and Anna Fifield, "G20 to Look at Monetary Fund Initiative," *Financial Times*, March 9, 2010.

[9] The current account is the difference between exports and imports, plus net income payments and net unilateral transfers. By accounting identity, the current account is equal to net inflows of foreign capital. Current account deficits are financed by foreign capital inflows.

[10] IMF, *World Economic Outlook*, October 2009 and European Commission, DG Economic and Financial Affairs, *http://ec.europa.eu/economy*

[11] For example, see "A Very European Crisis," *Economist*, February 4, 2010.

[12] "Country Report: Greece," *Economist Intelligence Unit*, April 2010.

[13] http://ec.europa.eu/economy

[14] For more about the effects of the global recession on government budgets, and how governments have tried to address these challenges, see CRS Report R41 122, *Limiting Central Government Budget Deficits: International Experiences*, by James K. Jackson.

[15] "Is Greece Heading for Default?," *Oxford Economics*, January 29, 2010.

[16] For example, see Kerin Hope, Quentin Peel, and Tony Barber, "Greece Turns on EU Critics," *Financial Times*, February 13, 2009 and Louise Story et al., "Wall St. Helped to Mask Debt Fueling Europe's Crisis," *New York Times*, February 14, 2009.

[17] "Fiscal Woes to Dog Greek Bonds Even if Aid Offered," *Reuters*, March 22, 2010. 10 basis points = 0.1 percentage point.

[18] Carrick Mollenkamp and Cassell Bryan-Low, "Greece Leaps One Key Hurdle," *Wall Street Journal*, March 5, 2010.

[19] Elena Becatoros and Melissa Eddy, "Greece Still Under Siege Despite Aid Pledge," *WTOP*, April 26, 2010.

[20] Economist Intelligence Unit, "Country Report: Greece," April 2010.

[21] At constant prices. IMF, *World Economic Outlook*, October 2009.

[22] *Update of the Hellenic Stability and Growth Programme*, Greek Ministry of Finance, January 2010, http://www.mnec.gr/export/sites/mnec/en/economics

[23] Ibid.

[24] Administration encompasses public services including: executive and legislative organs; financial and fiscal affairs; external affairs; foreign economic aid; general services; basic research; research and development; public debt transactions and other general services. "OECD Economic Survey: Greece," *OECD*, May 2007.

[25] International Monetary Fund, "Europe and IMF Agree €110 Billion Financing Plan With Greece," IMF Survey online, May 2, 2010.
[26] "OECD Economic Survey: Greece," *OECD*, July 2009.
[27] Economist Intelligence Unit, "Country Report: Greece," March 2010; OECD Economic Survey: Greece, July 2009; and Hellenic Foundation for Foreign and European Policy (ELIAMEP), *Economic Fact Sheet Greece 2009/10*, March 2010.
[28] "Is Greece Headed for Default?," *Oxford Economics*, January 29, 2010.
[29] *Resolution of the European Council on the Stability and Growth Pact*, Amsterdam, June 19, 1997, *Council Regulation (EC) 1466/97*, and *Council Regulation (EC) 1467/97*, http://ec.europa.eu/economy
[30] European Commission, *Report from the Commission: Greece*, Brussels, May 19, 2004, http://ec.europa.eu/economy
[31] European Commission, *Recommendation for a Council Decision Abrogating Decision 2004/91 7/EC 9 on the Existence of an Excessive Deficit in Greece*, Brussels, May 16, 2007, http://ec.europa.eu/economy 12_commission_en.pdf.
[32] European Commission, DG Economic and Financial Affairs, *Stability and Growth Pact, Country-specific procedures*, http://ec.europa.eu/economy
[33] On April 22, 2010, the EU's statistical authority, Eurostat, estimated the Greek government's 2009 budget deficit as 13.6% of GDP, almost one percentage point higher than the 12.7% of GDP previously estimated by the Papandreou government.
[34] For more details on the Greek government's proposed austerity measures, see Greek Ministry of Finance, *Update of the Hellenic Stability and Growth Programme*, January 2010; and *Report to the Implementation of the Hellenic Stability and Growth Programme and Additional Measures*, March 2010. Both available at *http://www.mnec.gr/en/economic s/growth*
[35] "Greece Economy: An Austere Future," *Economist Intelligence Unit*, March 9, 2010.
[36] "Greece/EU: Athens Frets under Financial Supervision," *Oxford Analytica*, February 17, 2010. A 2008 reform of the Greek pension system legally reduced the number of pension funds from 133 to 13 (with five basic funds and eight smaller and supplementary funds). However, some observers have noted that the 2008 reforms have yet to be fully implemented.
[37] European Commission Economic Forecast for Greece, Spring 2010, May 5, 2010, http://ec.europa.eu/economy "Country Report: Greece," *Economist Intelligence Unit*, April 2010.
[38] Hellenic Foundation for Foreign and European Policy (ELIAMEP), *Economic Fact Sheet Greece 2009/10*, March 2010; "Is Greece Heading for Default?," *Oxford Economics*, January 29, 2010.
[39] Hellenic Foundation for Foreign and European Policy (ELIAMEP), *Economic Fact Sheet Greece 2009/10*, March 2010.
[40] "Athens Upbeat After Aid Talks with IMF Chief," *ekathimerini .com*, April 26, 2010.
[41] IMF, "Frequently Asked Questions: Greece," May 11, 2010. http://www.imf.org/external/ np/exr/faq/ greecefaqs.htm#q23.
[42] Andrew Willis, "Greek Loans Will Be Ready in Time, EU Says," *euobserver.com*, May 4, 2010, http://euobserver.com/19/30007.
[43] The IMF has "preferred creditor status," meaning that IMF member states give priority to repayment of their obligations to the Fund over other creditors. The United States has never lost money on its commitment to the IMF
[44] IMF, "IMF Quotas," March 11, 2010, http://www.imf.org/external/np/exr/facts/quotas
[45] IMF, "IMF Reaches Staff-level Agreement with Greece on €30 Billion Stand-By Arrangement," press release, May 2, 2010, *http://www.imf.org/external/np/se c/pr/2010/pr10176.htm.*
[46] "Rebuilding Greece's Finances," *Economist*, February 4, 2010.
[47] "Rebuilding Greece's Finances," *Economist*, February 4, 2010.

[48] Charles Wyplosz, "And Now? A Dark Scenario," VoxEU, May 3, 2010, http://www.voxeu.org/index.php?q=node/4987.
[49] Arvind Subramanian, "Greek Deal Lets Banks Off the Hook," *Financial Times*, May 6, 2010.
[50] Ibid.
[51] Sergio Goncalves and Axel Bugge, "ECB Gives Greece Verbal Support, Dashes Rescue Hopes," *ABC News,* May 6, 2010, *http://abcnews.go.com/Business/ wireStory? id=10572470.*
[52] Paul Krugman, "A Money Too Far," *New York Times*, May 7, 2010.
[53] Barry Eichengreen, "The Euro: Love It or Leave It?," VoxEU, November 17, 2007, *http://ww w.voxeu.org/index.php?q=node/729.*
[54] Bob Davis, "IMF's Reach Spreads to Western Europe," *Wall Street Journal*, May 10, 2010.
[55] Saleheen Khana and Kwang Woo (Ken) Park, "Contagion in the Stock Markets: The Asian Financial Crisis Revisited," *Journal of Asian Economics*, vol. 20, no. 5 (September 2009), pp. 56 1-569.
[56] Louise Story, Landon Thomas Jr., and Nelson D. Schwartz, "Wall St. Helped Mask Debt Fuelling Europe's Crisis," *New York Times*, February 14, 2010.
[57] Nelson D. Schwartz and Sewell Chan, "In Greece's Crisis, Fed Studies Wall St.'s Activities," *New York Times*, February 25, 2010.
[58] George A. Papendreou, *Remarks on Rising to the Challenge of Change: Greece, Europe, and the United States*, Brookings, March 8, 2010, http://www.brookings.edu/~/media
[59] Philip Whyte, "Why Christine Lagarde is Right About Germany," *Centre for European Reform*, March 26, 2010.
[60] Ibid.
[61] The G-20 is a forum for discussing economic policies among 20 major advanced and emerging-market countries. Following the financial crisis, financial regulation has been a major topic of focus at the G-20 meetings. For more on the G-20, see CRS Report R40977, *The G-20 and International Economic Cooperation: Background and Implications for Congress*, by Rebecca M. Nelson.
[62] Wolfgang Münchau, "Why the Euro will Continue to Weaken," *Financial Times*, March 7, 2010.
[63] This effect was highlighted by Greece's Prime Minister in remarks at Brookings. See George A. Papandreou, *Rising to the Challenge of Change: Greece, Europe and the United States*, Brookings, March 8, 2010, http://www.brookings.edu/~/media
[64] For more on U.S.-EU economic ties, see CRS Report RL30608, *EU-U.S. Economic Ties: Framework, Scope, and Magnitude*, by William H. Cooper.
[65] Provisional data for end-2009 Q4. Bank for International Settlements (BIS), "Consolidated International Claims of BIS Reporting Banks," Table 9B: Consolidated Foreign Claims of Reporting Banks - Immediate Borrower Basis, http://www.bis.org/statistics
[66] For example, see Patrice Hill, "Bernanke Delivers Blunt Warning on U.S. Debt," *Washington Times*, February 25, 2010, and Anne Applebaum, "America's Debt Spiral Resembles Greece's Crisis," *Washington Post*, February 17, 2010.
[67] Mark Brown, Clare Connaghan, and Katie Martin, "Greek Bond Yields Spike to Record Levels," *Wall Street Journal*, April 22, 2010.
[68] Economist Intelligence Unit, "Country Report: Greece," April 2010.
[69] Kerin Hope, "Greece Passes Tough Austerity Measures," *Financial Times*, May 6, 2010.

In: International Debt in Individual Countries ISBN: 978-1-61761-787-4
Editors: Anthony L. Montefusco

Chapter 4

ARGENTINA'S DEFAULTED SOVEREIGN DEBT: DEALING WITH THE "HOLDOUTS"

J. F. Hornbeck

SUMMARY

In December 2001, following an extended period of economic and political instability, Argentina suffered a severe financial crisis, leading to the largest default on sovereign debt in history. It was widely recognized that Argentina faced an untenable debt situation that was in need of restructuring. In 2005, after prolonged, contentious, and unsuccessful attempts to find a mutually acceptable solution with its creditors, Argentina abandoned the negotiation process and made a one-time unilateral offer on terms highly unfavorable to the creditors. Although 76% of creditors accepted the offer, a diverse group of "holdouts" opted instead for litigation in hopes of achieving a better settlement in the future. Although Argentina succeeded in reducing much of its sovereign debt, its unorthodox methods left it ostracized from international credit markets for nearly a decade and triggered legislative action and sanctions in the United States.

Argentina still owes private creditors $20 billion in defaulted debt and $10 billion in past-due interest, as well as $6.2 billion to Paris Club countries. Of the disputed privately held debt, U.S. investors hold approximately $3 billion. The more activist investor groups have lobbied Congress to pressure Argentina to reopen debt negotiations. Some Members of Congress have introduced punitive legislation in both the 110th and 111th Congress, but to date it has not received any legislative action. Nearly five years after the original debt workout, however, a confluence of circumstances has persuaded Argentina to restructure the holdout debt, particularly the need to secure long-term public financing.

On April 15, 2010, Argentina announced the key features of the proposed bond deal, which will be made in a formal offer on April 30, 2010. Argentina expects to complete the process in June 2010. Two offers are proposed, one for retail (small) investors, the other for institutional (large) investors. Retail investors will receive replacement bonds for the full face value of the defaulted bonds they currently hold. Past due interest will be paid in cash. Institutional investors will receive a discount bond equal to a 66.3% reduction in the face value of the defaulted debt they currently hold (the so-called "haircut"). Past due interest will be covered by a separate seven-year "Global" bond. Interest rates vary depending on the bond. Both groups of investors will receive a GDP-linked security called a warrant that provides for additional payments should the Argentine economy grow at rates higher that anticipated and stipulated in the final prospectus. Analysts value the deal at between 48 and 51 cents on the dollar, compared to 60 cents for the 2005 exchange.

For Argentina, a successful restructuring requires a sufficiently large participation rate to eliminate most of the existing judgments and attachment orders. Argentina expects, with no guarantee, that such an outcome will lead to renewed access to the international credit markets. Historically, sovereign debt workouts with at least a 90% participation rate have achieved this goal. Since holdouts compose 24% of the original bondholders, a 60% participation rate of this group would allow for the total participation rate to reach the 90% threshold, including the 2005 exchange. If the exchange succeeds, Argentina will have completed a sovereign debt restructuring with the deepest write-off of principal in history. Many original bondholders were severely hurt by this deal, as was Argentina by the crisis. Secondary market participants may see a sizable profit. If there is a legacy to the Argentine case, it may be in the changes to bond contracts that seek to improve outcomes for creditors. One option is the use of collective action clauses (CACs), now standard for sovereign debt, which require all creditors to bargain collectively, with a compulsory majority decision applicable to all bondholders.

INTRODUCTION

In December 2001, following an extended period of economic and political instability, Argentina suffered a severe financial crisis, leading to the largest default on sovereign debt in history. In 2005, after prolonged, contentious, and unsuccessful attempts to find a mutually acceptable solution to restructuring the debt, Argentina abandoned the negotiation process and made a onetime unilateral offer on terms highly unfavorable to creditors. Although 76% of them accepted the offer, a diverse group of "holdouts" opted instead for litigation in hopes of achieving a better settlement in the future. Argentina still owes private bondholders $20 billion in defaulted debt and $10 billion in past-due interest. It is also in arrears to the United States and other governments on $6.2 billion in loans. Although Argentina succeeded in reducing much of its sovereign debt, its unorthodox methods have left it ostracized from international credit markets for nearly a decade and triggered legislative action and sanctions in the United States.

The lingering effects of the debt default became a legacy problem for Argentina, but in October 2009, the Argentine government decided to restructure the remaining holdout debt. Argentina made the necessary filings at the U.S. Securities and Exchange Commission (SEC) and its European and Japanese counterparts for a debt exchange. Following a number of internal political complications that delayed the process, a formal approved offer will be made April 30. Taking into consideration all aspects of offer, financial analysts value it at 48-51 on the dollar, compared to 60 cents for the 2005 exchange. It remains to be seen how large a response this offer will bring and whether it is sufficient to allow Argentina to achieve its primary goal of being able to renew borrowing in the international credit markets.

BACKGROUND TO THE CURRENT DEBT RESTRUCTURING

Argentina's 2001 debt crisis resulted from many factors. For the most part, Argentina fell victim to its own economic policies, but these were compounded by questionable lending and policy advice by the International Monetary Fund (IMF), a global recession, and international credit markets determined to chase high-yielding debt with inadequate regard to risk. Together, these factors propelled Argentina toward a position of unsustainable debt that ended in an unprecedented default and restructuring scheme.

The 2001 Financial Crisis

Argentina's 2001 financial crisis has its roots in a history of untamed fiscal policy, the Achilles' heel of Argentine economic strategy for most of the 20th century. Argentina has long relied on fiscal largesse as a basic policy tool, covering its shortfalls by printing currency or relying on more creative alternatives to expand the money supply. This approach to fiscal governance, as would be expected, led to recurring bouts of high inflation and indebtedness, typically followed by temporary efforts to stabilize prices. In the 20th century, such a policy culminated with the hyperinflation of 1989-90, which toppled the Alfonsín government, bringing Carlos Menem to the Presidency along with his well-known Minister of Economy, Domingo Cavallo.[1]

The Menem-Cavallo cure for chronic inflation was the now infamous "convertibility plan." Enacted on April 1, 1991, it set the stage for the crisis that would emerge a decade later. The plan legally guaranteed the convertibility of pesos to dollars at a one-to-one fixed rate and limited the printing of additional currency only to amounts supported by its reserve position (which could fluctuate with the amount of dollars entering or leaving the country). Upholding this promise, however, required that monetary and fiscal policies also be constrained—the money supply could not be expanded to cover deficits. Therefore, to preserve this system, deficits either had to be eliminated or financed through debt.

At first convertibility worked well; it forced fiscal and monetary discipline on the government, which combined with strong economic growth, reduced inflation and debt service. Cracks in Argentina's economic policy, however, soon began to appear. The main problem was that fiscal deficits were not contained at either the provincial or national levels to thresholds required to support the convertibility plan. By 1993, debt began to grow, compounded by the practice of rolling it over. From 1995 to 2001, the debt service ratio grew from 30% to 66%.[2] The Argentine peso soon became greatly overvalued, reducing Argentina's competitiveness and ability to export, with predictable declines in public revenue.

Fiscal balances further deteriorated with a strengthening dollar (to which the peso was linked), competitive devaluations by its major regional trading partners (most importantly Brazil), and falling commodity prices. Argentina was already entering a four-year recession when the global downturn arrived in 1999, causing public revenue to fall further. The weaknesses of the convertibility plan's strict policy constraints were now exposed. It has been likened to a straitjacket precisely because the Argentine government had no policy room to address the recession. The convertibility plan, by definition, prohibited devaluing the peso to increase exports, and excessive debt eliminated the option for a fiscal stimulus to counter the economic downturn. The third option, reducing government spending, only guaranteed a deeper recession. By this point, there was already little chance of Argentina avoiding financial disaster.[3]

In retrospect, it is also clear that in addition to Argentina's policy choices and an increasingly hostile global economy, actions by the international community were complicit in deepening the severity of Argentina's financial crisis. Global credit markets lent generously to Argentina, even after risk factors began to rise to worrisome levels. Investment bank and credit agency reports overstated Argentina's strengths.[4] Also, the IMF agreed to numerous lending arrangements made between 1991 and 2001 based on promised changes in Argentine policies and economic assumptions and projections that ranged from being overly optimistic to unrealistic. U.S. policy for much of the time could not be divorced from those of the IMF. Without the IMF, the convertibility plan would have collapsed much sooner. By its own admission, the IMF made repeated mistakes in surveillance, conditionality, and economic analysis that resulted in lending too much for too long into an untenable situation. Many economists would later argue that Argentina would have been better off had the IMF ended its support and pushed for debt restructuring much earlier.[5]

Notwithstanding the many factors that compounded Argentina's financial problems, the government's economic policies were the major cause of the economic crisis. Faced with the unsustainable situation described above, and falling international credibility, Argentina was unable to roll over its debt. Financial panic and political unrest ensued. On December 20, 2001, President de la Rua resigned and six days later, a new government defaulted on Argentina's sovereign debt. Soon thereafter the government abandoned the convertibility plan and devalued the peso. The Argentine default left the government in arrears with a number of international creditors. It owed private investors \$81.8 billion, the Paris Club countries \$6.2 billion,[6] and the IMF \$9.8 billion. Addressing the large private-sector debt was Argentina's most pressing problem, which was undertaken in a highly unusual manner.

The Debt Restructuring of 2005

The severe financial crisis hit Argentina hard. Between capital flight and the large peso devaluation, much of the country's wealth evaporated nearly overnight. Poverty and unemployment skyrocketed, leading to street protests and political unrest. As Argentina turned to address its debt problem, it argued that bondholders would have to share in the misery that affected the whole country, and that the government had a moral duty to ensure this outcome. It was, as many argued, a matter of equity that the write-down on bonds be historically high, particularly given that continued lending from the IMF, investment banks, and foreign governments at a time when it was clear that Argentina faced an impending crisis had only compounded the financial problems. Perhaps most importantly, Argentina was simply in no position to repay such massive debt.[7]

A sovereign default means the government is no longer willing or able to pay the debt it has incurred in the international markets. Sovereign defaults occur periodically and are typically worked out in what amounts to a consensual understanding between creditors and debtors. This type of understanding usually takes the form of a debt restructuring, which involves a formal and legal change in the contractual arrangements of the debt, such as reducing the face value of the obligations, issuing new bonds with lower interest rates and longer maturities, and capitalizing overdue interest, usually at a sizable loss to bondholders. Historically, a "successful restructuring" typically has had a 90% or greater participation rate (there are always some holdouts) by offering no less than 50% on the net present value of the debt. Usually, this process unfolds with the assistance of the IMF in setting macroeconomic targets that form the basis for a mutual understanding of a country's ability to repay its debt.[8]

Argentina began the debt restructuring process in 2002, negotiating with the IMF and investors for three years to find a solution that it felt was commensurate with its deeply diminished economic and social reality. Facing a huge debt burden, Argentina adopted a hard line toward all parties, insisting on a large write-down of principal for private creditors and postponing action on Paris Club and IMF debt. After years of negotiation, which were criticized by both sides, Argentina eventually determined that it had reached an impasse with creditors and decided to act on its own. It suspended its agreement with the IMF and filed for a one-time unilateral offer with the SEC to settle with private creditors. The Argentine legislature codified this commitment, passing the so-called "Lock Law" (Ley Cerrojo), which prohibited the government from reopening the exchange or making any kind of future offer on better terms. This action served the dual purpose of ensuring participating bondholders would not lose out on any better deal in the future, and thereby enticed a relatively higher participation rate than might otherwise have been the case.[9]

On January 14, 2005, Argentina opened the bond exchange for six weeks hoping to reach a final settlement on the $81.8 billion face value of debt plus $21.4 billion of past due interest (PDI). The default was unprecedented for its size ($103.2 billion), lengthy resolution (over three years), low recovery rate (30% on a net present value basis, including PDI), and large residual holdout (24% of creditors). Bondholders and the IMF criticized Argentina for engaging in a process that stretched (creditors would argue flaunted) the accepted guidelines of sovereign debt negotiations. Nonetheless, of the $81.8 billion face value of debt, $62.2 was exchanged for $35.2 billion of new bonds. The Argentine government, however, was unable to settle the matter fully because $19.6 billion of bonds (24% of eligible securities) were not tendered and remained in dispute along with accrued interest, $6.2 billion of Paris Club arrears, and $9.8 billion of IMF debt.[10]

Argentina has addressed this remaining debt in one of two ways. In 2006, it decided to repay in full the $9.8 billion owed to the IMF, relieving the government of any pressure to follow IMF policy constraints. Alternatively, Argentina has so far declined to restructure or repay debt owed to the Paris Club countries or holdouts. Holdout creditors have pursued litigation to force repayment, with the resulting judgments and attachment orders effectively precluding Argentina from borrowing in the international capital markets until the defaulted bonds are repaid or restructured.[11] For years, neither of these responses affected Argentina's determination to deviate from its policy of "financial independence." Strong economic growth until the 2008 global financial crisis and reliance on various stop-gap measures (details below) to meet financing gaps have allowed Argentina to rebuff attempts at forced resolution.

Argentina made a first effort to restructure the remaining defaulted debt in September 2008. As President, Cristina Fernández de Kirchner announced that Argentina would seek to repay the Paris Club debt out of its approximately $47 billion of international reserves and signed an agreement with a three-bank consortium (Barclays Capital, Deutsche Bank, and Citibank) to consider their offer to renegotiate with private holdout creditors. The simultaneous onset of the global financial crisis, however, put an end to the potential deal and any hope of meeting short-term financing needs with international borrowing.[12]

U.S. Responses to Argentina's Debt Repudiation

Argentina owes approximately $29 billion of bond principal and interest arrears to private investors and $6.2 billion of loans to Paris Club countries, including nearly $500 million in arrears to the United States. Private bondholders, the United States Government, and Members of Congress have each taken actions to encourage Argentina to repay these debts.

Private Sector Responses

In the eyes of institutional creditors, the 2005 Argentine restructuring set a precedent that could not be condoned, even though a majority of bondholders accepted the terms. Although Argentina continues to argue that the restructuring was a negotiated solution, it was not a mutually agreed one. Bondholders had to accept or reject the offer with the alternative being no restitution at all. Some holdouts sought legal remedies in the United States and other countries, as well as at the World Bank's International Center for the Settlement of Investment Disputes (ICSID). In the United States, 158 suits have been filed, 18 of which are class actions.[13] Creditors argued that Argentina had not fulfilled its obligations under either the bond contracts or its bilateral investment treaty with the United States.

Because many bonds in the hands of holdouts are still being traded, ownership is difficult to track. They were originally marketed in local country currencies: 58% in Euros, 38% in U.S. dollars, 2% in Argentine pesos, and the remaining 2% in other currencies. U.S. ownership is still estimated at approximately $3 billion. Funds that have brought suit against Argentina in U.S. courts have made claims on $2 billion of principal.[14] Because most of these funds are legally organized in countries known for their lack of financial transparency, it is difficult to state with certainty the nationality of ownership.[15]

Depending on the owner of the bonds, the goal of the litigation strategy differs. Institutional funds representing corporate and investment banks generally seek improved terms on the exchange.

Funds representing retail (individual) investors, mostly European, also have held out for a better settlement. Hedge funds and so-called "vulture funds," which purchase risky assets in the secondary market at highly discounted prices, typically sue for full recovery. Their "holdout" strategy can be highly profitable for investors with patience, realizing capital gains on undervalued bonds, often purchased after the default, and potentially receiving full restitution of interest and principal if the holdouts dwindle to a sufficiently small percentage of the total unresolved debt.[16]

Litigation has applied considerable leverage on Argentina, even without reaching some final point of resolution. It has, nonetheless, resulted in $8.6 billion in legal judgments and attachment orders from U.S. courts, which has precluded Argentina from raising funds in the international credit markets.[17] For example, approximately $105 million of Argentina's Central Bank reserves are frozen in the Federal Reserve Bank of New York and another $2 billion of global bonds backing guaranteed loans are on hold at the Depository Trust Company.[18] On January 12, 2010, a U.S. judge froze $1.7 million of Argentine central bank reserves held at the Federal Reserve Bank of New York because the Fernández government attempted to use them to guarantee payment of debt coming due in 2010, thereby making them eligible for attachment (see below).

Because the Argentine government did not recognize any creditor groups as negotiating partners, the hedge and "vulture" funds have also served as one form of admittedly imperfect investor coordination. While they bring greater pressure to bear on Argentina because of their collective action, their prolonged delaying tactics in seeking full restitution can clash with other investors wishing to purse a settlement strategy.[19]

U.S. Government Responses

With Argentina's default on Paris Club debt, including nearly $500 million owed to the United States government, a number of sanctions have been invoked automatically as defined in U.S. law. U.S. agencies are prohibited from lending to a country that is in arrears on its debt to the U.S. government including the Export-Import Bank, Overseas Private Investment Corporation, and the U.S. Trade and Development Agency. The U.S. military is prohibited from offering Foreign Military Financing, exercising the Excess Defense Articles through 505 Drawdown authority, or fully using the Global Peacekeeping Operations Initiative funding. In addition, all foreign assistance is prohibited except for International Military Education and Training funding and certain programs related to countering terrorism and trafficking in narcotics or persons.[20]

Legislative Responses

In Congress, some Members have responded to U.S. creditor concerns with the introduction of punitive legislation against Argentina. The Judgment Evading Foreign States Accountability Act of 2009 (H.R. 2493) was introduced in the 111th Congress on May 19, 2009, and driven in part by the American Task Force Argentina (ATFA), a private lobby group representing various constituents, including hedge and "vulture funds."[21] The bill cites Argentina's decision to ignore judgments against its actions as detrimental to U.S. investors and undermining the United States legal system. The bill's stated goal is to protect future investors by motivating those countries identified as "judgment evading foreign states" to "raise their standards of behavior." It would deprive such states and any state-owned corporations from issuing debt in the U.S. capital markets and would require that any future debt offerings carry written warnings that they have failed to satisfy outstanding judgments against them. The bill would also require that any request for bilateral or multilateral assistance be accompanied by a statement identifying the country as a "judgment evading state." To date, Congress has not acted on this bill.

Table 1. Argentina: Total Public Sector Debt, 2009 (in $ billions)

Debt Category	Amount	Percent
Performing Debt:	**133.9**	**79.0%**
Bonds and Bills	91.2	
Loans and Other	42.7	
Other	0.5	
Nonperforming Debt:		
Private ("holdout"):	**29.2**	**17.3%**
Falling Due	5.2	
Past Due:		
Principal	15.0	
Interest	9.0	
Paris Club:	**6.2**	**3.7%**
Principal	5.1	
Interest	1.1	
Total Public Sector Debt	**169.8**	**100.0%**
Total Public Debt/GDP	59.4%	

Data Source: Institute of International Finance and Government of Argentina, Ministry of Economy and Public Finances.

Despite lack of congressional action on H.R. 2493, the Government of Argentina has expressed a strong reaction against it, in part because it is directed at the actions of a single country and viewed from Argentina, amounts to a threat of imposing economic sanctions. The Argentine embassy has indicated that passage of such a bill could lead to a deterioration of bilateral relations, although there has been relatively little attention paid to the legislation in general.

ARGENTINA'S DEBT PROFILE AND RATIONALE FOR RESTRUCTURING (AGAIN)

As may be seen in **Table 1**, the portion of "holdout" debt plus that owed to the Paris Club represents 21% of Argentina's total public sector debt. For eight years, Argentina has been unable or unwilling to find a solution that would restructure this portion of debt, but circumstances have changed. Argentina has both the political will and financial incentives to negotiate a final solution to its long-outstanding debt issue.

There are three major incentives for Argentina to resolve its outstanding debt issues. First, in the medium to long run, Argentina, like many countries, will need to borrow in the international capital markets. Although its financing gap for fiscal year 2010 is reportedly covered, the steep decline in 2009 fiscal revenue relative to expenditures points to a deteriorating fiscal position. The fiscal balance has fallen from a surplus of 1.4% of gross domestic product (GDP) in 2008 to an expected deficit of -0.7% of GDP in 2009 (see **Appendix A**). By initiating a restructuring process now, when financial requirements are not an immediate threat, Argentina may have the time to make the political and financial arguments for reengaging the international credit markets at reasonable rates.[22]

Second, opportunities for ad hoc financing may be limited. In the absence of access to international capital markets, Argentina has met its financial needs by placing debt with domestic government agencies, restructuring domestically held debt, selling bonds directly to the government of Venezuela, and nationalizing private pension funds. In a recent example, on December 14, 2009, President Fernandez attempted to create a $6.6 billion Bicentennial Fund for Stability and Debt Reduction. The fund would have set aside money to guarantee early repayment for debt coming due in 2010. While on the surface it may seem to reinforce Argentina's commitment to meet its debt service, it presented numerous problems because the commitment would be financed from Central Bank reserves, which the government would purchase with 10-year government bonds. In addition to undermining the independence of the Central Bank, this strategy would have diminished Argentina's international reserve position and allowed the government to defer difficult decisions on fiscal adjustment.[23]

Using Central Bank reserves to guarantee debt payments is an unusual move and was challenged by both the president of the Central Bank of Argentina, who refused to transfer the funds, and the Argentine Congress. President Fernández responded with a presidential decree dismissing the Central Bank President and he resigned his position on January 29, 2010. Nonetheless, the Argentine courts suspended application of the presidential decree to finance the Bicentennial Fund, deciding that the congress must vote on the matter. President Fernández later rescinded the original decree, replacing it with two others in an attempt to avoid a constitutional problem in using Central Bank reserves to guarantee Argentine multilateral and private sector obligations coming due.[24]

Third, market conditions are favorable for placing debt. Interest rates are low by historical standards and liquidity is high and there may be ample appetite for Argentina's higher yielding bonds. Recent uncertainty surrounding the Bicentennial Fund, however, have caused bond yields to rise, making the proposed bond swap and any future debt offerings relatively more expensive for the Argentine government.

By some measures, Argentina is also in better financial shape to address repudiated debt than it was during the 2001 crisis or the 2005 restructuring. Argentina has a positive current account balance and has increased its international reserves from $10.4 billion in 2002 to $47.5 billion in 2009. During the 2003-2008 economic recovery, Argentina had an average annual growth rate of 8.5% and the increased revenues have until recently allowed it to maintain a primary surplus of 2.8% or higher (for detailed data, see **Appendix A**.) The primary surplus reflects the fiscal surplus after non-debt expenditures have been paid, and so is a measure of resources available exclusively for debt service. Because of the global financial crisis, however, the primary surplus fell to 1.2% of GDP in 2009, levels inadequate to reduce Argentina's total public debt, and its medium-term fiscal capacity remains in question unless it is able to return to the credit markets.

RESTRUCTURING THE HOLDOUT DEBT

A sovereign debt restructuring is a complicated matter and in Argentina's case the government faced three core and interrelated issues in attempting to form a strategy to: (1) negotiate a solution with private debt holdouts; (2) repay or reschedule Paris Club debt; and (3) reengage the IMF. It was widely believed that a successful conclusion for Argentina was unlikely without meeting all three goals to some degree, in part because they are interrelated. First, the Paris Club generally does not entertain a sovereign debt restructuring proposal without the debtor country undergoing an Article IV review of its economy (standard practice for all IMF country members), and having an IMF lending program in place. Among other goals, the Article IV review provides one presumably unbiased assessment of Argentina's economic health and ability to repay its debt, although Argentina has been particularly distrustful of the institution since the 2001 crisis. The IMF, however, usually does not consider a formal program until the "holdout" creditors have been offered a proposal.

The IMF review can be important in part because it can affect a country's borrowing rates. There was, however little hope for a clean IMF review for Argentina at this time. Among other issues, the IMF has registered grave concerns over the politicization of Argentina's economic data reporting. The national office of statistics, Instituto Nacional de Estadística y Censos (INDEC), has been criticized in particular for misrepresenting national inflation data.[25] The discrepancy can be seen in Appendix A. By underreporting increases in price levels, the Argentine government can reduce public sector costs by, for example, having lower inflation-based price adjustments where applicable and borrowing domestically at artificially lower nominal interest rates. Correcting data reporting is important for making a valid assessment of Argentina's ability to pay future debt obligations. More recently, INDEC has been reforming its statistical reporting methods, but recent estimates suggest it is capturing only 70% of total inflation[26] and the IMF is unlikely to provide a fully positive review of Argentina if this problem is not corrected.

These issues raised two important questions: was Argentina willing to accede in whole or in part to these requirements, and if so, what is the sequence that would make the most sense to ensure that all three conditions are met? As it turned out, Argentina skirted the entire issue, moving ahead with the bond exchange without an IMF review and promising to deal with the Paris Club at some future date.

For Argentina, a "successful" restructuring requires a sufficiently large participation rate to eliminate most of the existing judgments and attachment orders. Argentina expects, with no guarantee, that such an outcome will lead to renewed access to the international credit markets. Historically, sovereign debt workouts that involve a 90% voluntary participation rate or higher have been able to achieve this goal. A participation rate of 60% or higher of the holdout group would allow for the total participation rate, including the 2005 participants, to reach this threshold. Reportedly, the three-bank consortium organizing the offer represents 40%-50% of the holdouts. Therefore, Argentina would need only an additional 10%-20% of holdouts to reach this goal. Given that there are many funds that have acquired their Argentine bonds in the secondary market at highly depressed prices, it is possible that they would be willing to exchange these bonds, allowing the 90% threshold to be achieved.

THE 2010 PROPOSED EXCHANGE

In 2009, Argentina began the initial process of setting up a new bond exchange, taking three important steps: (1) President Cristina Fernández de Kirchner lent full support for the deal; (2) on November 18, 2009, the Argentine legislature suspended that portion of the 2005 law that prohibited reopening a debt restructuring offer; and (3) in December 2009, the Argentine government filed a preliminary prospectus with the SEC, which approved Argentina's request to issue new bonds. On April 15, 2010, the Minister of Economy announced the key features of the proposed bond deal. A formal offer will be made on April 30, 2010. An early tender for institutional investors will be open May 3-12, 2010, while the general submission will open on June 7.

The proposed exchange is structured so to provide different offers for two separate categories of bondholders: small retail investors, defined as those holding less than $50,000 of defaulted bonds, and institutional investors, or those holding amounts greater than $50,000, a feature also present during the 2005 exchange. The retail investors will receive a more generous offer to entice their support in order to ensure a minimally acceptable overall participation rate.

The bond exchange must address two aspects of outstanding debt. First, the face (or par) value of the bond. This term refers to the stated value on the bond when it was issued. Second, it must address past due interest (PDI), or the interest that has accrued since the default. In each case, both retail and institutional investors will receive a bond in exchange for the defaulted debt, cash or a separate "Global" bond for PDI, and a separate GDP-linked security called a warrant that provides for additional payments under certain circumstances (see **Table 2** for a summary of the bond characteristics).

Face Value

Retail investors will be offered a par bond in which they will be compensated for the full face value of the bonds they hold. Total par bonds are limited to $2 billion. Institutional investors, by comparison, must accept a 66.3% reduction in the face value of the bonds they hold. In each case, new bonds will be issued in exchange for the old ones, with the discounted bond maturing in 2033 and carrying an annual interest rate of 8.28%. Par bonds will mature in 2038, carry a sliding annual interest rate beginning with 2.5% for the first 9½ years, 3.75% for the next 10 years, and 5.25% for the final 9½ years. Interest is paid semi-annually.

Table 2. Terms of Proposed Argentina 2010 Bond Exchange

Bond Characteristic	Retail Investors	Institutional Investors
Bond Type	Par Bond (pays full face value)	Discount Bond (66.3% reduction from face value)
Amount	$2.0 billion	$18.3 billion
Maturity Date	2038	2033
Annual Interest Rate	2.5%-5.25% increasing over time	8.28%
Past Due Interest	cash payment	Separate 2017 Global bonds @ 8.75%
GDP-linked warrant	yes, expiring by December 2035	yes, expiring by December 2035
2005 GDP Warrant Payments	no	no
Bank Commission	0.4%	0.4%

Source: Securities and Exchange Commission, *Amendment #5 to Argentina 18-K*, filed April 19, 2010.

Past Due Interest

Retail investors will be paid PDI in cash, covering interest from December 31, 2003 up to September 30, 2009. PDI for institutional investors will be covered by a par "Global" bond maturing in 2017 with interest paid in semi-annual interest payments, carrying an interest rate of 8.75%. It will cover interest from December 31, 2003 through December 30, 2009.

GDP-Linked Warrants

Both retail and institutional investors will receive GDP warrants, which will be securities that may be traded separately from the bonds to which they are attached. A warrant is a promise to make a particular offer under certain circumstances, often issued in connection to bonds to make them more attractive to investors. In this case, Argentina promises to make additional payments on the new bonds in the event that the Argentine economy grows faster than a predetermined and stated rate for any given year (to be outlined in the final prospectus). The warrant is meant to compensate for bonds outstanding in December 2001 and interest accrued to December 30, 2001, but payment in any given year is based on better than expected economic performance in the previous year. This feature turned out to be a particularly attractive feature of the 2005 exchange because Argentina emerged from its crisis with six years of high economic growth (see **Appendix A**), well above projected rates. Current estimates of Argentina's economic growth are considerably lower, which if accurate, would minimize the upside potential of this feature.

Investors had hoped that the new deal would include the equivalent of past payments on warrants issued in 2005, arguing that like past due interest, they are entitled to compensation from Argentina's better-than-expected fiscal position arising from very strong past economic growth. Argentina decided not to include such payments, reasoning that the holdouts had declined to participate in that growth. Because these previous warrant payments help offset the heavy discount taken by institutional investors, there is some debate as to whether their absence from the 2010 exchange will affect the participation rate.

Valuation

In the arcane world of bond valuation, analysts estimate the value of the proposed exchange for discount bonds at between 48 and 51 cents per dollar value of the bond. These numbers compare unfavorably with the 60 cents on the dollar valuation of the 2005 exchange, which included a better than expected performance because of GDP-linked warrants.[27] Analysts estimate that inclusion of past payments of GDP warrants would have added 7 cents on the dollar to the offer. The defaulted bonds are currently trading around 49-50 cents on the dollar in the market, nearly four times their lowest trade level of 11 cents recorded in September 2008.[28]

OUTLOOK

Argentina may be on the verge of finally completing, largely on its own terms, the restructuring of the largest and most controversial default on sovereign debt in history. There was little disagreement that in 2002 Argentina faced a desperate financial situation that required a radical restructuring of debt, including a large write-off by bondholders. The historical precedent for such an outcome has been set on many occasions. The Argentine debt restructuring framework, however, involved methods, processes, and a deep discount that were notably unprecedented. In addition, although Argentina negotiated for years with creditors under IMF guidelines, it ultimately made a "take it or leave it" offer, with the promise that no better offer would be made.

Argentina has kept its promise by making a proposed 2010 bond exchange that is valued below the 2005 offer. Much of the debt, however, has been trading on the secondary market, at prices as low as 11 cents on the dollar, so there may be opportunity for many institutional investors, including the "vulture funds," to gain on a transaction valued at between 48 and 51 cents on the dollar. The 2010 offer is widely expected to draw sufficient support to exchange most of the remaining defaulted debt. Analysts estimate that this could lead to over 90% of total defaulted debt being exchanged, including the 76% tendered in the 2005 workout.

There is some likelihood that a small percentage of investors will not accept these terms and prefer to let the litigation option play out. Court reactions to these holdouts are not easy to predict, but technically any judgments against Argentina would still be in place for untendered defaulted bonds.

In the end, Argentina's debt restructuring was costly for all parties, raising a lingering question of whether it represents a new template for debtor countries in the future. For many reasons, it arguably does not. Perhaps the major lesson for Argentina is that a prolonged disregard for fiscal responsibility can have dramatic long-term economic, social, and political consequences. At the financial level, the costs to Argentina have been severe, particularly its inability to access international credit markets. This cost was compounded by Argentina's resorting to creative, but unorthodox financing mechanisms that could not adequately replace conventional financial arrangements. If the new debt restructuring allows Argentina access to international credit, the bonds likely will carry higher interest rates than those of many other countries. This situation does not seem like a desirable model for other countries contemplating a sovereign default.

The Paris Club so far has also been a loser in this case. The Argentine case demonstrates that national governments may be limited in their efforts to influence a sovereign nation that is determined to delay or deny debt repayment. For the United States, neither sanctions nor legislative proposals have had any noticeable influence on Argentina, and actually may have reinvigorated Argentina's resolve to stay the course of default as long as possible. In the end, it was the international markets that appeared to have the greatest leverage on Argentine decision making.

Creditors also clearly suffered, with the exception of those with the patience and willingness to accept the risk of purchasing highly discounted debt in the secondary markets. Creditors as a whole are best served by a quick and mutually-agreed debt workout, which historically has led to better and more equitable terms than those offered by Argentina. The lack of collective action presented a serious problem in this case. The financial markets have since responded in ways that seek to avoid a second occurrence of a prolonged, costly, unilateral workout.

The most important development along these lines is the adoption of collective action clauses (CACs) in virtually all sovereign debt. These clauses allow for a majority of bondholders to bargain collectively and require a minority holdout group to capitulate to the majority negotiated solution. They have become the "market standard" for sovereign bonds governed by the laws of New York, typically where foreign debt is placed in the United States, including Argentina's.[29] While it is not possible to compensate most of the original bondholders of Argentine debt in this case, it is likely that CACs and other bondholder cooperation mechanisms will improve chances for better outcomes in the future. CACs may help investors negotiate for better returns in the case of a future default and also likely reduce the holdout problem, eliminating the need for "vulture" funds, which often trade on the losses of other creditors and employ a strategy that can impede movement toward early resolution. Developments that improve investor coordination and more equitable outcomes in future defaults may be a major legacy of the Argentine debt crisis. It is no coincidence that both the 2005 and 2010 proposed exchange are governed by CACs.

APPENDIX A. ARGENTINA: SELECTED ECONOMIC DATA

Table A-1. Argentina Selected Economic Data, 2000-2009

	2000	2001	2002	2003	2004	2005	2006	2007	2008	2009
GDP Growth (%)	-0.8	-4.4	-10.9	8.8	9.0	9.2	8.5	8.7	7.0	0.7
Overall Fiscal Balance (%)	-3.6	-6.8	-2.0	0.9	3.7	2.1	1.9	1.1	1.4	-0.7
Primary Fiscal Balance (%)	0.4	-1.3	0.7	2.8	5.3	4.4	4.0	3.2	3.3	1.5
Inflation Rate INDEC (%)[a]	-0.7	-1.5	41.0	3.7	6.1	12.3	9.8	8.5	7.2	5.5
Inflation Rate others (%)								15.0	25.0	17.0
Current Acct Balance (% GDP)	-3.1	-1.4	8.5	6.3	2.1	2.9	3.6	2.8	2.1	na[b]
International Reserves ($ bn)	32.5	15.3	10.4	13.8	19.3	27.3	31.2	45.7	46.2	47.5
Public Debt (% GDP)	45.7	53.7	166.4	138.7	127.3	73.9	64.0	56.1	48.8	59.0
Internat'nal Bond Issues ($ mn)[c]	13,468	2,711	0	100	200	540	1,896	3,256	65	na[b]

Source: United Nations Economic Commission on Latin America and the Caribbean (ECLAC). *Estudio Económico de América Latina y el Caribe 2008-2009*, July 2009 and Government of Argentina, Ministry of Economy and Public Finances (for debt figures).

Notes

a. Instituto Nacional de Estadistica y Censos – Argentina's official government statistical office, which has come under criticism for grossly understating inflation rates since 2007. Adjusted inflation rates have been added on the line below to reflect private sector estimates of annual inflation rates since 2007

b. na = not available

c. Includes sovereign, financial sector, and other commercial debt.

End Notes

[1] Gerardo della Paolera, Maria Alejandra Irigoin, and Carlos G. Bózzoli, "Passing the Buck: Monetary and Fiscal Policies," in *A New Economic History of Argentina*, ed. Gerardo della Paolera and Alan M. Taylor (Cambridge: Cambridge University Press, 2003), pp. 72-74. Inflation hit a high of nearly 200% per month in 1990 and as noted by these and other authors, high inflation is costly. It reduces the real value of money with the resulting loss of purchasing power equivalent to a large "inflation tax" on society as a whole.

[2] Ibid., and CRS Report RS21072, *The Financial Crisis in Argentina*, by J. F. Hornbeck. Debt service ratio = public sector debt/exports.

[3] Ibid, pp. 2-4. Argentina required a more, not less, competitive exchange rate to attract foreign currency needed for debt service. As long as the peso was pegged to an appreciating dollar, this was not possible, and with the addition of a procyclical fiscal policy, Argentina eventually was unable to cover its debt obligations.

[4] Paul Blustein, *And the Money Kept Rolling in (And Out): Wall Street, The IMF, and the Bankrupting of Argentina.* (New York: Public Affairs, 2005), pp. 5-8, 31-35, 198-200.

[5] The dominant view at the IMF, despite some strong internal opposition, was that the IMF could not abandon Argentina for fear of being viewed as the cause of its economic collapse. Ibid, pp. 100-106, 134, 140-41, 157 and CRS Report RL32637, *Argentina's Sovereign Debt Restructuring*, by J. F. Hornbeck.

[6] The Paris Club is a voluntary, informal group of 19 creditor nations who have agreed to act with a common approach to negotiate debt relief for developing countries unable to meet their external obligations. Members of the Paris Club agree to restructure and/or reduce official debt owed to them on a case-by-case basis, provided certain conditions are met. See, CRS Report RS21482, *The Paris Club and International Debt Relief*, by Martin A. Weiss.

[7] Juan Pablo Bohoslavsky and Kunibert Raffer, "¿Qué Hacer con los Reclamos de los Acreedores Holdouts?," *Economía*, January 24, 2008 and Universidad de Buenos Aires. Plan Fénix. *La Argentina y su Deuda Externa: En Defensa de los Intereses Nacionales.* July 2004. http://www.econ.uba.ar/planfenix.

[8] For examples of five recent developing country defaults that had participation rates of 93%-98%, see: Marcus Miller and Dania Thomas, "Sovereign Debt Restructuring: The Judge, the Vultures, and Creditor Rights," *The World Economy*, vol. 30, no. 10 (October 2007), p. 1497.

[9] The Republic of Argentina, *Registration Statement No. 333-163784*, Securities and Exchange Commission, Washington D.C., April 9, 2010, p. 4. This document also contains Argentina's view of the crisis and 2005 exchange.

[10] CRS Report RL32637, *Argentina's Sovereign Debt Restructuring*, by J. F. Hornbeck. p. 11-13 and Fitch Ratings. *Argentina: Rapprochement with Creditors and Sovereign Ratings.* Special Report. November 19, 2009, p. 2.

[11] Argentina's international bonds were issued under eight different jurisdictions, including New York and a number of foreign countries. Some 38% of the untendered bonds were denominated in U.S. dollars. Those issued under the jurisdiction of the State of New York are subject to U.S. law. Miller and Thomas, "Sovereign Debt Restructuring: The Judge, the Vultures, and Creditor Rights," pp. 1492-1493, 1496, and 1502.

[12] Jude Webber, "Argentina Mulls Delay to $6.7 billion Debt Repayment," *Financial Times*, October 11, 2008.
[13] The Republic of Argentina, *Registration Statement No. 333-163784*, Securities and Exchange Commission, Washington D.C., April 9, 2010, p. 11.
[14] Correspondence with U.S. Department of State, January 12, 2010.
[15] A few funds are legally incorporated in the United States, the rest in the Cayman Islands, British Overseas Territories, Turks and Caicos, British Virgin Islands, Switzerland, and Luxembourg. *Main Judgments and PreJudgment Claims Against the Argentine Republic*, provided by the Embassy of Argentina, December 2009.
[16] Miller and Thomas, "Sovereign Debt Restructuring: The Judge, the Vultures, and Creditor Rights," p. 1497.
[17] There are 158 judgments against Argentina and many include attachment orders in which the courts can seize funds from any future debt that might be issued by Argentina, effectively prohibiting access to the international credit markets. A list of claims against Argentina is summarized in, *Main Judgments and Pre-Judgment Claims Against the Argentine Republic*, provided by the Embassy of Argentina, December 2009.
[18] Correspondence from U.S. Department of State, January 12, 2010.
[19] Amrita Dhillon, Javier García-Fronti, Sayantan Ghosal and Marcus Miller, "Debt Restructuring and Economic Recovery: Analysing the Argentine Swap," *The World Economy*, vol. 29, no. 4 (April 2006), pp. 392-393.
[20] Correspondence from U.S. Department of State, January 12, 2010.
[21] Ibid., and Mark Weisbrot, "Vulture Funds Lobby Against Argentina," *America Latina en Movimiento*, August 6, 2009. http://alainet.org/index.phtml
[22] The official Argentine position stresses that the need for financing is not the major incentive for restructuring its debt, but fiscal reality argues to the contrary. Ministerio de Economía y Finanzas Públicas. *Boudou Explicó en Diputados los Alcances de la Suspensión de la Ley Cerrojo*. October 28, 2009.
[23] International Monetary Fund, *Global Markets Monitor*, Washington, D.C., December 16, 2009, p. 4.
[24] Jude Webber, "Argentina Debt Battle Intensifies," *Financial Times*, January 11, 2009, p. 3 and Volkel, Christian, "Government Appeals Against Suspension of Argentine Debt Payment Fund, *IHS Global Insight*, February 8, 2010.
[25] Helen Parsons, Carola Sandy, and Igor Arsenin, *Argentina: Rising Tide Lifts All Boats*, Credit Suisse, New York, NY, September 17, 2009, p. 1.
[26] International Monetary Fund, *Global Markets Monitor*, Argentina, December 14, 2009, p. 4.
[27] Igor Arsenin and Carola Sandy, *Argentina's Debt Swap Offer: Good Enough*, Credit Suisse, New York, April 15, 2010, p. 1.
[28] International Monetary Fund, *Global Markets Monitor*, April 16, 2010, p. 5.
[29] Michael Waibel, "Opening Pandora's Box: Sovereign Bonds in International Arbitration," *The American Journal of International Law*, vol. 101, no. 4 (October 2007), p. 736.

In: International Debt in Individual Countries ISBN: 978-1-61761-787-4
Editors: Anthony L. Montefusco

Chapter 5

THE FEDERAL GOVERNMENT DEBT: ITS SIZE AND ECONOMIC SIGNIFICANCE

Brian W. Cashell

SUMMARY

After several years of surpluses in the late 1990s, the federal budget has been in deficit since FY2001. Deficits represent the additional borrowing required in each year to bridge the gap between tax revenues and spending outlays. Each deficit adds to the already existing stock of outstanding federal debt.

Some of those deficits may have seemed large at the time, but the budget deficit for FY2009 was unprecedented, in dollar terms, and the FY2010 deficit is also expected to be much larger than those of past years. The prospect of such rapid growth in the federal debt may seem alarming, and some might wonder how much the debt can grow before it poses significant economic risks.

In a slack economy, federal borrowing and spending can stimulate growth in output in the short run. As the economy approaches full employment, federal government borrowing adds to total credit demand and tends to push up interest rates. Higher interest rates increase the cost of financing new investment in plant and equipment and thus may tend to reduce the stock of productive capital below what it might otherwise have been. That would tend to reduce the long-run rate of growth.

In the long run, the relationship between the growth rate of the federal debt and the overall rate of economic growth is critical to economic stability. As long as the debt grows more rapidly than output, the ratio of debt to gross domestic product (GDP) will rise. Debt growth in excess of economic growth is ultimately unsustainable. Whether the debt-to-GDP ratio is on such a path depends on the size of the budget deficit, the rate of interest, and the rate of growth in GDP.

What matters most, as far as economic stability is concerned, is what investors believe to be the long-run outlook for the debt-to-GDP ratio. If large deficits are expected to persist, or if the interest rate on the debt is expected to exceed the growth rate indefinitely, then at some point the federal government may begin to find it more difficult to sell new securities.

Should the federal government be unable to find private sector buyers, the Federal Reserve might buy Treasury securities in order to sustain their marketability. Should it decide to do so, then the threat is no longer one of government insolvency, but rather of inflation.

INTRODUCTION

After several years of surpluses in the late 1990s, the federal budget has been in deficit since FY2001. Deficits represent new borrowing required in each year to bridge the gap between tax revenues and spending outlays. Each deficit adds to the already existing stock of outstanding federal debt.

Some of the deficits in recent years may have seemed large at the time, but the budget deficit for FY2009 was unprecedented, in dollar terms, and the deficit in FY2010 is expected to be considerably larger than in past years as well. The prospect of such rapid growth in the federal debt may seem alarming, and some might wonder how large, or how rapidly, the debt might grow before it poses significant economic risks.

One way in which policymakers have expressed their concerns over the level of federal government debt is in the form of a statutory debt limit.[1] Although the debt limit tends to rise as necessary, those increases serve as occasions to consider the debt itself separately from the policies that account for it.

There is more than one measure of federal debt, and that may be a source of confusion. This chapter explains the different measures of the U.S. government debt, discusses the historical growth in the debt, identifies the current owners of the debt, presents comparisons with government debt in other countries, and examines the potential economic risks associated with a growing federal debt.

MEASURING THE FEDERAL DEBT

The statutory debt limit is a ceiling set by Congress restricting the total amount of federal debt outstanding. Gross federal debt, with some minor adjustments, is the measure that is subject to the limit.

Although gross federal debt is the broadest measure of the debt, it may not be the most important one. Not all of the gross debt actually represents past borrowing in credit markets. Some of the debt is held by the so-called trust funds, primarily the one for Social Security, but also others such as unemployment insurance, the highway trust fund, and one for federal employee pensions. Relatively small amounts of debt are also held by selected federal agencies.

The assets held by the trust funds consist entirely of non-marketable federal debt. That debt exists only as a bookkeeping entry, and does not reflect past borrowing in credit markets. The trust fund balances represent the cumulative amount that the government has not had to borrow in credit markets since they were simply credited to the trust fund accounts.[2]

The debt measure that is relevant in an economic sense is debt held by the public. This is the measure of debt that has actually been sold in credit markets, and which has influenced interest rates and private investment decisions. At the beginning of calendar 2010, the debt held by the public was $7.8 trillion, whereas total gross federal debt was $12.3 trillion.

The dollar amount of the debt, however large it may seem to be, is not the best measure of its burden on the economy. Just as an individual with a larger income can afford to take on more debt, the importance of the debt can only be measured relative to the overall size of the economy.[3] For a given amount of debt, the larger the potential tax base is, the less of a burden on the economy the interest payments on that debt will be. The most common way of putting the size of the debt in perspective is to express it as a percentage of total gross domestic product (GDP).

RECENT HISTORY OF THE FEDERAL DEBT

Prior to World War II, the federal budget was in surplus about as often as it was in deficit. Some of the largest increases in the debt resulted from wartime spending. There were large increases in the debt held by the public related to the Civil War and also to World War I. Since World War II, the federal budget has been in deficit most of the time and the debt has steadily grown. Since 1940, revenues exceeded outlays in only 12 years.[4]

Figure 1 shows gross federal debt held by the public since 1940. The red line plots the dollar value of the debt held by the public since 1940. These are nominal amounts (i.e., they have not been adjusted for inflation). The black line shows the debt held by the public as a percentage of GDP.

The dollar value of the debt rose gradually until the late 1970s and early 1980s, at which time its growth accelerated. It peaked in 1997, fell through 2001, but since then has reached a new high each year. Measuring the debt relative to GDP tells a different story. The surge in debt to finance the costs of World War II is much more pronounced and indicates that recent debt levels are far from unprecedented, in terms of the burden to the economy. Following that surge and until the late 1970s, however, debt grew much less rapidly than did the overall economy and so the ratio fell steadily. Between 1980 and 1995, the debt grew more rapidly than the economy so the ratio rose. Between 1995 and 2001, with the decline in debt levels, the ratio fell. Between 2002 and 2005, it rose again, but then fell in 2006 and 2007 even with significant deficits. It is above the recent peak reached in 1993 but, for now, it is below what it was in 1955. Given current projections the debt-to-GDP ratio seems likely to continue to rise over the next few years.

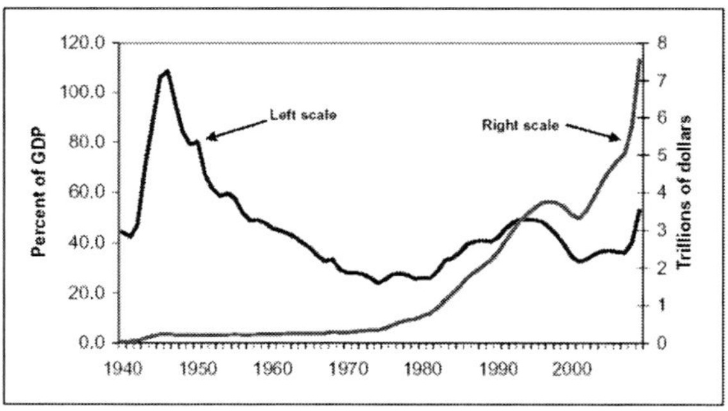

Source: Congressional Budget Office.

Figure 1. Federal Debt Held by the Public.

THE SHORT- AND LONG-RUN EFFECTS OF FEDERAL BORROWING

In the short run, growth in the public debt (i.e., budget deficits) affects the composition of economic output. When there is considerable slack in the economy, the main effect of an increase in the deficit may be to stimulate demand and raise output. That's the reasoning behind the fiscal stimulus in the American Recovery and Reinvestment Act of 2009 (P.L. 111-5).

Eventually, however, as the economy approaches full employment, and credit markets tighten, federal government borrowing tends to push up interest rates. Higher interest rates increase the cost of financing new investment in plant and equipment and thus may tend to reduce the stock of productive capital below what it might otherwise have been. Thus, there may be a shift in the composition of output towards consumption and away from investment. Consumption that might otherwise have been deferred (i.e., saving) is reduced and current consumption rises.

The higher interest rates may also have an effect on international capital flows, and thus on the trade balance. Other things being equal, they make dollar-denominated assets more attractive to foreign investors because of the relatively higher yield. Foreign investors, in order to buy U.S. securities, must first buy dollars with which to pay for them. The increased demand for dollars in exchange markets tends to push up the price of the dollar in terms of other currencies.[5]

The increase in the exchange value of the dollar has two mutually reinforcing effects. First, the price of imported goods falls because it takes fewer dollars to buy the same quantity of goods and services abroad. Lower prices for imported goods means, other things being equal, that U.S. consumers spend more on goods and services produced abroad. Second, the price of U.S.-produced goods and services rises for foreigners because the amount of foreign currency required to buy a given quantity of U.S. exports rises. Because U.S. exports are more expensive, they tend to decline.

Both the rise in imports and the drop in exports contribute to a larger trade deficit. Because of the increased domestic borrowing associated with the rising federal debt, firms that sell a significant share of their production abroad, and those that compete directly with foreign firms selling in the United States, experience a drop in the demand for their goods and services. The increased capital inflow, however, may offset to some extent the reduction in investment that might otherwise result from the increase in domestic credit demand.[6]

WHO OWNS THE FEDERAL DEBT?

Because Treasury securities are seen as relatively safe, they are held by a wide range of investors. Next to cash they are the most liquid asset, meaning they can easily be converted to cash when necessary, on short notice. Because of that, investors hold them as a way of managing the overall risk associated with their portfolios.

Figure 2 shows a breakdown of the holders of the outstanding gross federal debt. The U.S. government is itself the largest holder of the debt, mainly in the trust funds. Included in the "other" category are financial institutions, including banks, insurance companies, and mutual funds, as well as private pension funds. The Federal Reserve holds a significant share of the debt. The Federal Reserve buys and sells Treasury securities in its open market operations in order to manage short-term interest rates.[7] State and local governments hold Treasury securities as well, mainly in pension funds for their employees. Foreign investors hold 29.3% of the debt.

The Treasury Department publishes estimates of major foreign holdings of Treasury securities. Mainland China, Japan, and the United Kingdom are the three largest holders. **Table 1** presents recent data for countries with the largest holdings of Treasury securities.

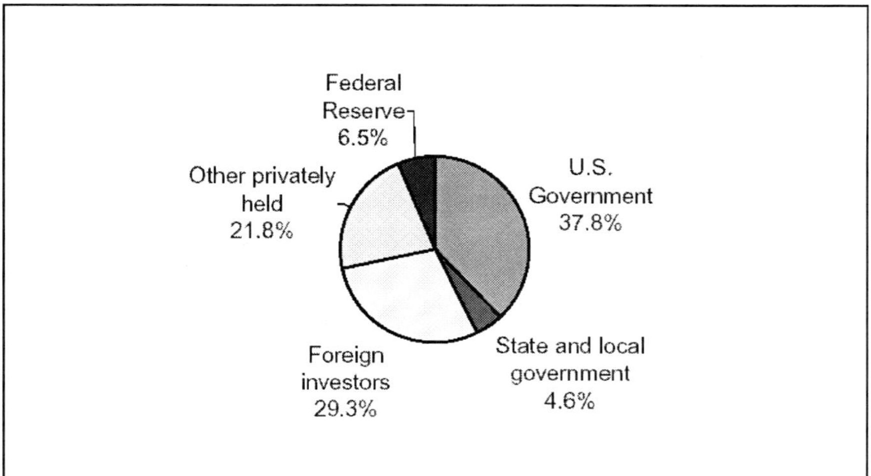

Source: Department of the Treasury.

Figure 2. Ownership of the Gross Federal Debt, June 2009.

Table 1. Major Foreign Holders of Treasury Securities as of November 2009

Country	Holdings (billions of dollars)	Percentage of Foreign Held Debt
Total Foreign Held	3,597.5	100.0
Mainland China	789.6	21.9
Japan	757.3	21.1
United Kingdom	277.5	7.7
Oil Exporters	187.7	5.2
Caribbean Banking Centers	179.8	5.0
Brazil	157.1	4.4
Hong Kong	146.2	4.1
Russia	128.1	3.6
Luxembourg	91.7	2.5
Taiwan	78.4	2.2
Switzerland	63.0	1.8
Germany	53.6	1.5

Source: Department of the Treasury; Federal Reserve Board.

Notes: Oil Exporters include Ecuador; Venezuela; Indonesia; Bahrain; Iran; Iraq; Kuwait; Oman; Qatar; Saudi Arabia; the United Arab Emirates; Algeria; Gabon; Libya; and Nigeria.

THE RELATIONSHIP BETWEEN FEDERAL DEBT AND GDP

In the long run, the relationship between the growth rate of the federal debt and the overall rate of economic growth is critical to economic stability. As long as the debt grows more rapidly than output, the ratio of debt to GDP will rise. Perpetual debt growth in excess of economic growth is inherently unsustainable.

Whether the debt-to-GDP ratio is on such a path depends on the budget deficit, of course, but also on the rate of interest and the rate of growth in GDP.[8] To illustrate, consider the case where the budget is balanced except for the interest payment on the debt. In other words, the budget deficit is equal to the interest payment. In this case, the debt would grow each year by an amount equal to the interest cost of financing the debt. Thus, the growth rate of the debt would equal the interest rate. If the interest rate were higher than the growth rate of GDP, then the debt would grow faster than GDP and the ratio of debt to GDP would rise. If, instead, the interest rate stays below the economic growth rate, then the ratio of debt to GDP would fall.

Figure 3 compares the average interest rate on the federal debt with the growth rate of nominal GDP. This measure of economic growth reflects changes in both real output and inflation. The green line shows the annual growth rate of nominal GDP, and the red line shows the average interest rate on the outstanding federal debt held by the public.

For most of the period between 1940 and 1980, the interest rate remained well below the growth rate of the economy. For much of the past 25 years, however, the interest rate has been above the growth rate, which through the mid-1990s contributed to the rising debt-to-GDP ratio. If the interest rate is less than the growth rate, it is possible for the debt ratio to fall even with a modest budget deficit. When the interest rate is above the growth rate, a surplus is required to keep the debt-to-GDP ratio from rising.

Consider the case where the budget deficit is larger than the interest payment on the debt. When the budget deficit is larger than the interest payment, the difference between the two is sometimes referred to as the "primary" deficit. In that case, the growth rate of the debt would be larger than the interest rate, and so, even with an interest rate below the GDP growth rate, the debt-to-GDP ratio could still rise. **Figure 4** shows the relationship between the budget deficit and the interest payment on the debt from 1940 through 2009. The black line shows the deficit (which in some cases is negative, i.e., a surplus), and the red line shows the interest payment.

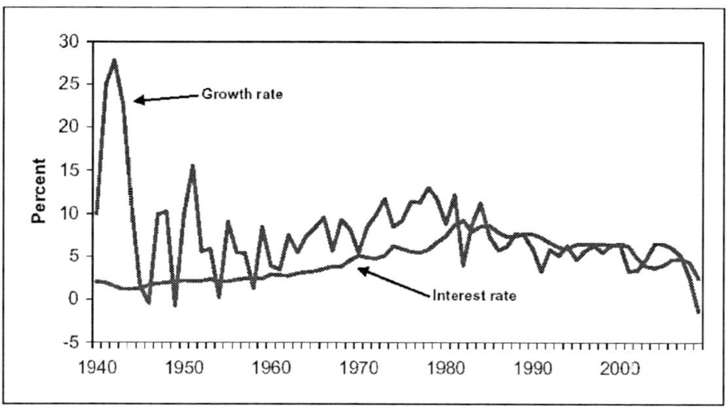

Source: Department of Commerce, Bureau of Economic Analysis; Congressional Budget Office.

Figure 3. Economic Growth and Interest on the Federal Debt.

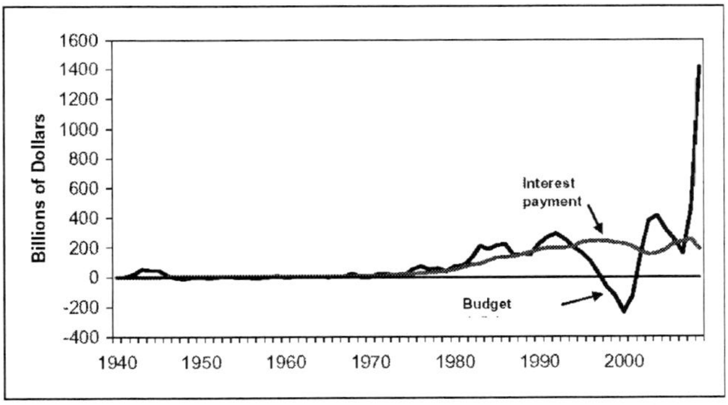

Source: Congressional Budget Office.

Figure 4. The Budget Deficit and Net Interest Outlays.

Although there were clearly exceptions, the overall pattern until recently was for the budget deficit and the interest payment to rise in tandem, which is not surprising since the deficits represents additional debt which requires a larger interest payment. In the late 1990s, when the budget was in surplus (i.e., a negative deficit), the budget deficit was clearly substantially less than the interest payment which contributed to the decline in the debt-GDP ratio. Since FY2003 that situation has reversed, and except for FY2007 the deficit has been larger than the interest payment.

WHAT ARE THE RISKS OF RISING FEDERAL DEBT?

The federal government usually has little difficulty in marketing securities when revenues fall short of outlays. As long as there is a ready market for federal debt, the risks are small.

What matters most, as far as economic stability is concerned, is what investors believe the long-run trend in the debt-GDP ratio to be. If large primary deficits (deficits in excess of the net interest payment) are expected to persist, or if the interest rate on the debt is expected to exceed the growth rate indefinitely, then at some point the federal government may find it more and more difficult to sell new securities. In other words, it may become harder for the federal government to find willing lenders to finance its deficits. At worst, private investors might come to doubt the federal government's ability even to meet its interest payments, and would be reluctant, if not completely unwilling, to hold government bonds.

Inability to borrow money in credit markets can be fatal to private businesses. Firms that are losing money and cannot find willing lenders are on the road to bankruptcy. The federal government, however, has a source of credit not available to individual businesses, the Federal Reserve Bank.

There are two possible outcomes should the federal government be unable to find private sector buyers, either domestic or foreign, for its securities. First, the federal government could simply find itself unable to meet all of its obligations. In that case outlays would have to fall unless taxes were increased enough to eliminate the shortfall. Second, rather than allow the government to default, the Federal Reserve might buy sufficient Treasury securities in order to sustain their marketability.[9]

Although subject to congressional oversight, the Federal Reserve is independent and under no legal obligation to ensure the sale of government securities. But should it decide to do so, then the threat is no longer one of government insolvency, but rather of inflation.

When the Federal Reserve buys Treasury securities, it increases the stock of reserves to commercial banks. Those increased reserves, in turn, increase the banks' capacity to lend money and create demand deposits, increasing the stock of money in circulation. The historical record demonstrates that continued financing of large government budget deficits by "printing money" runs a substantial risk of rapidly accelerating inflation.

Current and projected federal debt, however, are both short of the levels thought to be associated with this risk. For the moment, federal debt remains well below the level it reached following World War II.

History provides a number of examples where large public sector debt led to serious economic consequences. In the aftermath of World War I, four countries experienced episodes of rapid inflation directly attributable to the central bank financing of very large budget deficits through money creation: Germany, Poland, Austria, and Hungary. In each of these cases, more than one-half of the total central government expenditures was deficit financed. As a result, the public lost confidence in the governments' ability to bring growth in public sector debt under control by either raising taxes or cutting expenditures.[10]

Immediately following World War II, Hungary experienced the most extreme episode of inflation on record. Between July 1945 and August 1946, the price level in Hungary rose by a factor of 3×10^{25}. As is characteristic of instances of very rapid inflation, tax revenues fell far short of public expenditures during this time. For much of the period, revenues covered less than 10% of total expenditures.[11]

During the mid-1980s, Bolivia experienced an episode of very rapid inflation. In 1984, general government revenues represented less than 20% of total government expenditures, and the budget deficit surpassed 20% of GDP. Annual inflation in 1984 was over 1,000%, and in 1985 the inflation rate topped 11,000%.[12]

These are all examples of extreme cases, but they serve to put the U.S. experience in perspective. Even in instances of much more modest federal government credit demand, there remains the possibility that the Federal Reserve might seek to mitigate any upward pressure on interest rates due to the Treasury's borrowing needs at the risk of pushing up the inflation rate. But as long as the Treasury can find buyers for its securities in private credit markets, the Federal Reserve will likely find it easier to pursue an anti-inflationary policy.

In any country with a large government debt there may be temptation to reduce the real value of that debt with inflation. In cases where that is perceived to be a real possibility, nominal interest rates may be higher than they otherwise would be because investors demand a higher rate of return to protect themselves from the possible decline in the value of their assets. The independence of the Federal Reserve is generally believed to reduce the possibility that will happen.[13]

GOVERNMENT DEBT IN OTHER INDUSTRIALIZED COUNTRIES

Short of the extreme examples cited in the previous section, it is useful to compare the federal government debt in the United States with that of other developed countries. The United States is not the only country whose central government has issued a significant amount of debt.

Among the countries shown in **Table 2** are all those participating in the European Economic and Monetary Union (EMU). These are the countries who now use the Euro as their currency. The Maastricht Treaty established conditions for European Union countries' participation in the EMU. Among them was the condition that a member country's public sector financial condition must be "sustainable." In particular, the standards for assessing the sustainability of public sector finances were that the public sector deficit not exceed 3% of GDP, and that the public sector debt not exceed 60% of GDP. More than half of the Euro countries now have debt-to-GDP ratios above 60%.

Table 2. Gross General Government Debt as a Percentage of GDP

Country	2000	2009
Austria[a]	71.1	72.9
Belgium[a]	113.8	101.2
Canada	82.1	82.8
Finland[a]	52.3	43.7
France[a]	65.6	84.5
Germany[a]	60.4	77.4
Greece[a]	114.9	114.9
Ireland[a]	40.2	65.8
Italy[a]	121.0	123.6
Japan	135.4	189.3
Luxembourg[a]	9.2	18.2
Netherlands[a]	63.9	71.4
Portugal[a]	62.0	83.8
Spain[a]	66.5	59.3
Switzerland	52.5	44.4
United Kingdom	45.1	71.0
United States	54.4	83.9

Source: Organization for Economic Co-operation and Development.

a. Member of the European Economic and Monetary Union (Euro country).

As the figures in **Table 2** indicate, the United States is far from having the largest government debt. Of the 17 countries shown, five had a higher debt-to-GDP ratio in 2009 than did the United States. Twelve countries increased their debt ratio between 2000 and 2009. Four of the countries had public debt larger than their GDP in 2009.

CONCLUSION

It appears that the federal debt is likely to rise significantly in the near future. The Congressional Budget Office now projects the budget to be in deficit through 2020. In the current economy, however, there is significant slack and debt growth is likely to affect aggregate demand much more than prices or interest rates.

At current and even at projected levels, most economists would agree the debt poses little immediate risk to economic stability. But continued deficits on the order of 10% of GDP eventually might, and are likely unsustainable. Ultimately the risk of a very large, and rapidly growing, government debt is extremely high rates of inflation, as pressure would mount on the Federal Reserve to monetize the debt.

End Notes

[1] CRS Report RL31967, *The Debt Limit: History and Recent Increases*, by D. Andrew Austin and Mindy R. Levit.

[2] Interest paid on the trust fund accounts is also strictly a bookkeeping entry and does not constitute an actual outlay of the federal government.

[3] Prospects for economic growth may also affect perceptions about the advisability of taking on more debt.

[4] See also CRS Report RL34712, *Ebbs and Flows of Federal Debt*, by Mindy R. Levit.

[5] In the current international economic environment a desire for quality investments may also affect capital flows. See CRS Report R40007, *Financial Market Turmoil and U.S. Macroeconomic Performance*, by Craig K. Elwell.

[6] In the longer run, as the amount of foreign holdings of U.S. assets increases, an increasing share of U.S. income will flow abroad in the form of interest, dividend, and rent payments. While this outflow does not necessarily mean a decline in U.S. living standards, it may mean that future living standards will not be as high as they would have been if a greater share of domestic investment had been financed by borrowing at home instead of abroad.

[7] Recently the share of Treasury securities held by the Federal Reserve has fallen. In an effort to add liquidity to credit markets, the Federal Reserve has swapped substantial amounts of Treasury securities for relatively riskier assets that were held by other financial institutions. See CRS Report RL34427, *Financial Turmoil: Federal Reserve Policy Responses*, by Marc Labonte.

[8] In the current discussion, both the growth rate and the interest rate are nominal (i.e., not adjusted for inflation).

[9] By law (section 14(b) of the Federal Reserve Act), the Federal Reserve can only buy Treasury securities in the open market. It cannot buy them directly from the Treasury.

[10] Thomas J. Sargent, "The Ends of Four Big Inflations," in Robert Hall, ed., *Inflation: Causes and Effects* (National Bureau of Economic Research, 1982), pp. 41-97.

[11] William A. Bomberger and Gail E. Makinen, "The Hungarian Hyperinflation and Stabilization of 1945-1946," *Journal of Political Economy*, vol. 91, no. 5 (1983), pp. 801-824.

[12] Juan-Antonio Morales, "Inflation Stabilization in Bolivia," in Michael Bruno et. al., eds., *Inflation Stabilization* (MIT Press, 1988), pp. 307-346.

[13] See CRS Report RL31056, Economics of Federal Reserve Independence, by Marc Labonte.

In: International Debt in Individual Countries ISBN: 978-1-61761-787-4
Editors: Anthony L. Montefusco

Chapter 6

IRAQ'S DEBT RELIEF: PROCEDURE AND POTENTIAL IMPLICATIONS FOR INTERNATIONAL DEBT RELIEF

Martin A. Weiss

SUMMARY

Following the ouster of the Saddam Hussein regime in spring 2003, Iraq's external debt was estimated to be around $130 billion. Reducing this debt to a sustainable level has been a priority of the U.S. government. Since 2003, debt relief negotiations have taken place in a variety of fora and led to the cancellation of a significant amount of Iraq's external debt.

Iraq's external debt comprised four components: Paris Club bilateral debt ($42.5 billion), non- Paris Club bilateral debt ($67.4 billion), commercial debt ($20 billion) and multilateral debt ($0.5 billion). Debt relief negotiations first led to an 80% reduction of the Paris Club debt. The Paris Club agreement also set the terms for non-Paris Club and commercial debt cancellation levels. A provision of the Paris Club agreement is that Iraq cannot accept a debt cancellation agreement with other creditors on more favorable terms for Iraq than those reached with the Paris Club. Thus, Iraq is expected to receive no more than an 80% cancellation from all of its creditors. Negotiations with non-Paris Club creditors are ongoing, and resolution of the commercial debt is largely complete.

The negotiations and process of providing debt relief to Iraq may shed some light on the approaches bilateral and corporate creditors take toward providing international debt relief to middle-income countries who would not be eligible for the debt relief already provided to the poorest countries. In light of Iraq's experience, three new precedents appear to have taken shape: (1) a willingness by the international community to grant a stay on the enforcement of creditor rights to collect unpaid sovereign debt; (2) an increased flexibility in Paris Club debt relief decisions; and (3) an unwillingness by successor regimes to claim that their debt is "odious" and repudiate it.

Iraq's debt relief has been a priority for both the Bush Administration and Congress. Debt relief is important to U.S. interests for several reasons, including releasing funds to help support Iraq's budget, pay for Iraq's security, and reestablish Iraq's financial standing with international creditors and the financial markets.

Iraq's Saddam-era debt is estimated at $130 billion and has been the focus of numerous negotiations over the past three years among bilateral, multilateral, and commercial creditors. These negotiations led to an 80% reduction of Paris Club and commercial debt.[1] Negotiations with non-Paris Club bilateral creditors including Saudi Arabia and other Persian Gulf countries are ongoing. The United States forgave its Saddam-era debt, worth $4.1 billion, in November 2004.

This chapter proceeds in three parts. The first provides a snapshot of the Iraq debt situation following the ouster of the Saddam regime. The second discusses subsequent debt relief negotiations and their resolution. The third presents three possible implications for future debt relief cases that arise from Iraq's experience. They are: (1) a willingness by the international community to grant a stay on the enforcement of creditor rights, (2) an increased flexibility in Paris Club debt relief decisions, and (3) an unwillingness by successor regimes to claim that their debt is odious and repudiate it.

IRAQ'S EXTERNAL DEBT

The precise dimensions of Iraq's foreign debt obligations are unknown. This is due to disagreements on what Iraq actually owes and how interest on this debt should be calculated (or if it should be counted at all).[2] Iraq's external debt following the end of the Saddam regime was approximately $130 billion. This debt comprised four components: official Paris Club bilateral creditors

($42.5 billion), official non-Paris Club bilateral creditors ($67.4 billion), commercial creditors ($20 billion) and multilateral creditors[3] ($0.5 billion). The first three major components are discussed below.

Paris Club Debt Claims

At the time of Iraq's Paris Club debt relief agreement on November 14, 2004, it was determined that Iraq's total external debt to Paris Club countries was $37.15 billion, including interest. [4] Later IMF estimates put the figure at $42.5 billion.[5] On July 10, 2003, the Paris Club issued a countryby-country breakdown of its member states' claims against Iraq. These figures are reproduced in **Table 1.**

Table 1. Total Iraq Paris Club Debt, 2003 (in U.S. $ millions, excluding interest)

Creditor Nation	Debt Owed
Japan	$4,108.6
Russia	$3,450.0
France	$2,993.7
Germany	$2,303.9
United States	$2,192.0
Italy	$1,726.0
United Kingdom	$930.8
Austria	$813.1
Canada	$564.2
Australia	$499.3
Spain	$321.2
Brazil	$192.9
Sweden	$185.8
Belgium	$184.5
Finland	$152.2
Switzerland	$117.5
Netherlands	$96.7
South Korea	$54.7
Denmark	$30.8
Total	**$20,917.9**

Source: The Paris Club

Iraq's debt to the United States consisted of loan guarantees issued between 1983 and 1993 by the U.S. Department of Agriculture for the sale of U.S. agricultural products to Iraq. Iraq defaulted on $2.19 billion of these guaranteed loans in 1991, just prior to the first Gulf War. The U.S. Department of Agriculture paid off the creditors and assumed the debt. By the end of the Saddam regime, accumulated interest increased Iraq's U.S. debt to approximately $4.1 billion.

Non-Paris Club Debt Claims

The majority of Iraq's external official debt is owed to non-Paris Club states. The IMF is the only definitive source for non-Paris Club debt and it has not made a country-by-country breakdown of this debt available. In the absence of such a breakdown, CRS has reviewed estimates compiled by Jubilee Iraq, an affiliate of the Jubilee organizations which campaign for international debt relief. These estimates are presented in **Table 2**. These are unofficial figures, representing only Jubilee Iraq's compilation of figures reported in the press, think tank reports, or official government remarks.[6]

Table 2. Non-Paris Club Debt (Various Estimates) (in U.S. $ million)

Creditor Nation	Debt Owed
Saudi Arabia	$30,000
Kuwait	$27,000
China	$5,800
Qatar	$4,000
United Arab Emirates	$3,800
Romania	$2,500
Serbia	$2,000
Turkey	$1,800
Bulgaria	$1,700
Jordan	$1,300
Poland	$564
Czech Republic	$147
Morocco	$32
South Africa	$24
Hungary	$17
India	$1

Source: Jubilee Iraq

Commercial Debt Claims

In 2003, Iraq's debt to commercial creditors was estimated to be $15 billion. In 2005, after further evaluation of claims by Iraq's government, the figure was raised to $20 billion. Commercial claims are geographically dispersed **(Figure 1)** and most claims are relatively small.[7] Of all the claims received, 36% of the claims were less than $1 million and 37% were between $1 and $10 million. U.S. dollar-denominated debt accounted for 72% of all claims, with the remainder denominated primarily in Japanese Yen (17%) and in Euros (8%).[8]

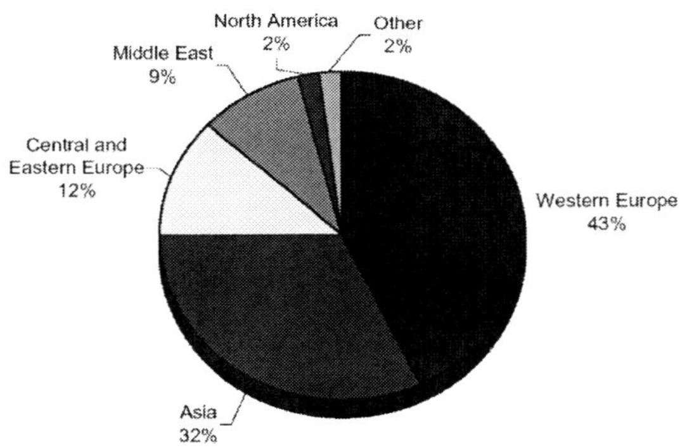

Source: Iraq Debt Collection Office

Figure 1. Regional Distribution of Iraq's Commercial Claims, 2005.

THE DEBT RELIEF EFFORT

Following the ouster of Saddam Hussein, the international community began the process of helping Iraq rebuild its economy.[9] An integral component of economic reconstruction following any conflict is resolving old debts and regaining access to the international financial community. Iraq, however, was a unique case. Unlike many of the world's poorest countries, Iraq is considered a middle-income country because of its substantial petroleum reserves. Iraq would likely be able to service its existing debts once its petroleum industry was functioning. Many analysts thus argued that Iraq appeared to be a good candidate for so-called "debt flow" treatment, involving rescheduling its official debts until it had the capacity to repay instead of cancelling them completely as is done for the poorest countries, which lack any natural resources that can be used to generate revenue. Others asserted that if Iraq's future oil revenues were used to fund repayment of old debts, not enough would remain to fund its current and future economic needs.

Discussion of cancelling Iraq's debt began soon after the ouster of the Hussein regime. Led by the Bush Administration, a consensus was reached that Iraq would receive debt relief on terms that were unique in light of its economic resources, but not unprecedented given the political situation. Debt relief has been provided to various countries for political and economic reasons. The United States, for example, has provided special bilateral debt relief to Egypt, Pakistan, Jordan, and Poland, among many other countries.

Paris Club Debt Relief

The Paris Club is an informal arrangement among creditor countries to abide by a fixed set of rules and principles for debt relief that have been agreed on by its members. Paris Club members meet periodically to reschedule, and in some cases collectively cancel, the debts owed to them by other countries. The U.S. share of any Paris Club debt relief must be appropriated by Congress.

Since the Paris Club was the most organized of all of Iraq's creditors, and included the major industrialized countries, it was able to start the debt relief negotiations and establish the precedents that other bilateral and commercial creditors would need to follow.

In September 2003, the G7 Finance Ministers called on the Paris Club "to make its best effort to complete the restructuring of Iraq's debt before the end of 2004."[10] President Bush appointed former U.S. Secretary of State James A. Baker III as his personal envoy on the issue of Iraq's debt in December 2003. Secretary Baker traveled to Europe, Asia, and the Middle East for discussions with foreign government officials in countries open to providing some debt relief to Iraq.

The Baker appointment, and the ensuing supportive response from other Paris Club countries, showed that the major creditor countries were interested in cancelling Iraq's external debt even though Iraq had the natural resources to eventually service its debts by itself. Prior to the Iraq case, Paris Club debt cancellation (rather than debt rescheduling) was only available for the poorest countries. Paris Club members began offering debt cancellation in addition to debt rescheduling in 1988. At the 1988 Toronto meeting of G7 Finance Ministers, Paris Club members agreed to extend to poor countries up to one-third forgiveness of their bilateral debts.[11] Over the next decade, the Paris Club gradually increased the amount of debt that it would be willing to cancel from 33.33% in 1988 to 90% in 1999.[12] Iraq, however, did not qualify for poor country debt relief due to its substantial petroleum reserves. Thus, Paris Club members would need to create a new framework, the Evian Approach, to cancel Iraq's debts.

Evian Approach

Strong Bush Administration support for Iraq debt relief likely contributed to the Paris Club's reshaping of its approach to debt relief in the runup to the 2003 Evian G8 Summit. The new Evian Approach introduces a new strategy for determining Paris Club debt relief levels that is more flexible and can provide debt cancellation to a greater number of countries then was available under prior Paris Club rules.

Instead of using economic indicators to determine eligibility for debt relief, as had previously been done, all potential debt relief cases are now divided into two groups: the heavily indebted poor countries (HIPC) and non-HIPC countries.[13] HIPC countries will continue to receive assistance under Cologne terms, which sanction up to 90% debt cancellation. All other countries will be assessed on a case-by-case basis.

Under the Evian Approach, a country seeking debt relief first undergoes an IMF debt sustainability analysis. This analysis determines whether the country suffers from a liquidity problem, a debt sustainability problem, or both. If the IMF determines that the country suffers from a temporary liquidity problem, its debts are rescheduled until a later date. If the country is also determined to suffer from debt sustainability problems, where it lacks the current resources to meet its debt obligations and the amount of the debt adversely affects its future ability to pay, the country is eligible for debt cancellation. During the Iraq discussions, Paris Club members determined that Iraq possessed an unsustainable amount of external debt, and began negotiating to cancel Iraq's debts.

Iraq's Paris Club Agreement

On November 21, 2004, the United States and other Paris Club members agreed on a debt relief program for Iraq providing a three-phase debt reduction of 80% of Iraq's external debts. Going into the Paris Club meeting to consider Iraq's debt, the United States was reportedly pressing for a 95% reduction of all of Iraq's debt to Paris Club members, while the Europeans, led by France and Russia, wanted only a 50% reduction. According to one press account,

Germany agreed to support a compromise figure of an 80% reduction, thus tipping the negotiations toward that figure.[14] According to the official Paris Club program, the terms of the Iraq deal are:

First Reduction: cancels 30% of the debt upon signing the bilateral agreements implementing the Paris Club agreement;

Second Reduction: cancels an additional 30% after an IMF program is signed; and

Third Reduction: cancels the final 20% of debt on completion of the last IMF Board review of three years of implementation of the IMF program.

When fully implemented, the Paris Club's treatment of Iraq's debt will reduce the total debt owed to Paris Club countries from $38.9 billion to $7.8 billion. This remainder (20% of the original total), will be rescheduled over a period of 23 years with an initial six-year grace period of repayments.

U.S. Debt Relief

On December 17, 2004, the United States forgave $4.1 billion (half principal and half interest)— 100% of the debt Iraq owed to the United States. However, since the United States writes off debt in net present value terms, not face value, the amount required was much less than the $4.1 billion. The fair market value of Iraq's debt was determined to be $360 million by the U.S. Treasury and was appropriated in a reallocation of financial resources for Iraq approved by Congress on September 29, 2004.

Table 3. Paris Club Debt Relief as of September 2008 in U.S. $ billion

Paris Club Creditors	Nominal Debt Stock
Before debt restructuring	$42.5
Debt relief to date of which:	$25.8
First debt reduction, end-2004	$14.3
Second debt reduction, end-2005	$11.5
Outstanding	$16.7

Source: IMF

Other Paris Club Country Debt Relief

Unlike the United States, most Paris Club members waited until Iraq signed an agreement with the IMF in December 2005 to implement their debt relief. Beginning in December 2005, remaining Paris Club members formally implemented their Paris Club debt relief agreement. The last Paris Club country to formally agree to a debt relief agreement with Iraq was Russia, which granted a debt reduction of 60 percent as of end-2005 on a reduced stock of debt of $4.5 billion on February 11, 2008.[15]

These agreements commenced the first two stages of Paris Club debt relief. In accordance with the Paris Club agreement under the new Evian Approach, 30% of bilateral debt would be immediately cancelled following signing the bilateral agreement and 30% would be cancelled following the signing of the IMF Agreement. The remainder of the debt would be cancelled following the successful completion of the IMF program.

Table 3 provides additional information on Paris Club debt relief to date:

Non-Paris Club Debt Relief

In some country debt relief negotiations conducted by the Paris Club, non-Paris club members participate on an ad-hoc basis. In the Iraq case, however, approximately two-thirds of Iraq's debt is held by non-Paris Club countries. Including those countries in the Paris Club negotiations may have been unfeasible and could have made a resolution much more difficult.

Arab creditor countries were not included in the Paris Club discussions, yet Iraq's Paris Club agreement required Iraq to seek terms that are at least equal to the debt relief negotiated with Paris Club members.[16] It may prove difficult to obtain such a high rate of debt cancellation from Iraq's non-Paris Club creditors. Moreover, since Paris Club debt relief came with strings attached in the form of IMF conditionality, it may be likely that non-Paris Club members will seek to attach conditions to any debt relief themselves, possibly in the form of preferential access to Iraqi oil, or other business and investment opportunities in Iraq.

During January 2004 meetings with representatives from Saudi Arabia, Kuwait, the United Arab Emirates (UAE), and Qatar—four Persian Gulf countries that, combined, hold approximately $65 billion of Iraq's debt—Secretary Baker received assurances that the Persian Gulf countries would significantly reduce their Iraq debt holdings once a sovereign Iraqi government was established.[17] Many observers suggest that Iraq's neighbors may want to wait on any final debt reduction until they see whether the future government in Iraq will be friendly to them. Arab creditors that are Iraq's Persian Gulf neighbors might also want more formal political arrangements to resolve

Sunni-Shiite disputes in Iraq on terms these creditors (all Sunni-ruled countries) would find sufficiently equitable.[18] To date, the only Gulf country to complete debt relief for Iraq is the UAE. On July 7, 2008, the UAE announced that it was fully writing off its remaining Iraq debt.[19]

In fall 2006, the Iraqi government, the United States, and several international institutions launched a development program to create an "International Compact with Iraq." The objective of the compact is to secure agreement from the Iraqi government to implement political and economic reforms in exchange for increased Arab debt relief and international aid contributions.[20] U.S. Secretary of State Condoleezza Rice initially raised the issue of Iraqi debt relief during discussions with Middle Eastern leaders in January 2007. In April 2007, Saudi Arabia reportedly acknowledged that it would provide debt relief of 80%, in accordance with the Paris Club agreement, although negotiations are continuing.[21] Since then, however, there has been no indication that debt relief is forthcoming from Saudi Arabia.

Iraq has resolved some of its smaller debts to non-Arab, non-Paris Club creditors. To date, Iraq has signed bilateral debt arrangements with eleven non-Paris Club creditors on terms comparable to the Paris Club agreement. According to the IMF, negotiations with Greece, Morocco, Tunisia, and the UAE have been concluded and debt agreements are expected soon. Debt relief negotiations with China and several other Persian Gulf countries are ongoing.

Table 4 provides summary information on non-Paris Club debt relief for Iraq.

Table 4. Non-Paris Club Debt Relief as of September 2008 (U.S. $ billion)

Non-Paris Club creditors (Concluded agreements only)	Nominal debt stock
Before debt restructuring	9.4
Debt relief to date	7.5
of which:	
Full cancellation	0.2
Cash settlement	5.4
On Paris Club terms	2.0
Outstanding	1.9

Source: IMF

Commercial Debt Relief

The final portion of Iraq's debt is commercial claims estimated at around $20 billion. These are outstanding commercial claims against various Iraqi guarantors that arose prior to the August 6, 1990 U.N. sanctions imposed when Iraq invaded Kuwait. The Iraqi government retained two U.S. companies, Ernst and Young and Citigroup, to adjudicate these debt claims and to help negotiate various settlements with small and large Iraqi creditors. The Iraq Debt Reconciliation Office was established in Amman, Jordan in May 2004.[22] On December 9, 2004, Iraq's Ministry of Finance posted an official query seeking information about commercial claims, including claims held by financial institutions, outstanding against the Iraqi government.

On July 26, 2005, Iraq announced the terms for its commercial debt renegotiation. For small creditors (less than $35 million), Iraq would settle claims through a cash buyback and cancellation. For larger claims, Iraq would seek a debt-for-debt swap. For small creditors, the cash purchase price would equal 10.25% of the outstanding claim up to a maximum of $4.3 million paid out. Larger creditors would receive, in line with the 80% debt cancellation requirement established by the November 2004 Paris Club agreement, new bonds carrying a face value of $200 for every $1,000 of their old debt. The new bonds are so-called "Eurobonds," arranged in London and trading in U.S. dollars. The bonds are guaranteed by the Iraqi government, will pay an annual coupon of 5.8%, and are due to mature in 2028.

The Eurobonds have been welcomed by investors and the exchange appears to have been successful. The bonds traded in the grey market prior to issuance at around 11% yield. This is an optimistic sign for the Iraqi economy. Several developing countries, such as Argentina and Brazil, were forced to pay much higher yields than Iraq did when they re-entered the bond market following their own recent economic crises.

Iraq concluded its commercial debt settlement in July 2006. A total of $19.7 billion of Iraqi commercial claims were settled as a result of four installments of the cash buyback offer for small debt holders, and two debt-for-debt exchanges.[23] Iraq reopened its commercial debt-restructuring program on January 30, 3008. According to the IMF, the offer appears to be successful and results should be published in the near future.

Potential Policy Precedents for International Debt Relief

As Congress considers new international debt relief arrangements, several precedents created by the Iraq case may be worth considering. In light of Iraq's experience, three new precedents appear to have taken shape: (1) a willingness by the international community to grant a stay on the enforcement of creditor rights to collect unpaid sovereign debt; (2) an increased flexibility in Paris Club debt relief decisions; and (3) an unwillingness by successor regimes to claim that their debt is odious and repudiate it.

Granting a Stay on the Enforcement of Creditor Rights

In the Iraq case, implementing a stay on the enforcement of creditor rights to use litigation to collect unpaid sovereign debt was a major priority and was implemented by U.N. Security Council Resolution 1483 shortly after the collapse of the Saddam regime. Implementation of this stay occurred with very little debate over whether such a comprehensive debt shield should be used.

In fact, a debate over the general advisability of debt shield mechanisms for countries facing economic crisis did occur between 2001 and 2003 at the IMF. At the time, there was concern that several South American countries, including Argentina and Brazil, would default on their international debts. During this debate, the U.S. Administration led the opposition to a comprehensive debt shield mechanism and the proposal was eventually withdrawn. It appears that after Iraq, however, such a debt shield mechanism is feasible if it is introduced in a political forum such as the United Nations rather than an economic/financial one like the IMF, and that it is an ad-hoc process, not attached to any formal mechanism for debt resolution.[24]

Sovereign bonds (government issued debt) are the primary form of developing country debt. These bonds are held by many types of investors, both large and small. The common issuance of sovereign debt represents a major shift in in how developing countries structure their debt. When countries ran into economic difficulties during the economic crises of the 1980s, their debts consisted primarily of bank loans issued by a small number of commercial banks. It was relatively easy for the banks to work together with delinquent countries and arrange terms to restructure the debt. There is now a much wider spectrum of investors in sovereign bonds, creating much costlier and more difficult resolutions. However, outside of the Paris Club, there is no formal mechanism to coordinate debt restructuring negotiations between creditors and the debtor government.

To address these concerns, in 2001, the IMF proposed creating the Sovereign Debt Restructuring Mechanism (SDRM) to help negotiate debt restructurings in general. Among other things, the IMF 's proposal was designed to afford rights to defaulting countries similar to those afforded bankrupt companies in the United States under Chapter 11 of U.S. bankruptcy codes. A stand-still on debt payments was to go into effect, while countries renegotiated their debt contracts with their creditors through a dispute resolution mechanism administered by the IMF. The debt standstill was considered one of the most important components of the proposed SDRM.[25] It also proved to be the one of the most highly contested issues concerning the SDRM proposal.[26]

The SDRM proposal was rejected by the Bush Administration, the private sector, and many Members of Congress. The Bush Administration advocated a more decentralized, market-oriented approach that would include clauses in sovereign bond contracts, known as Collective Action Clauses (CACs), which would stipulate how the financial contracts would be resolved pending a financial crisis or default.

A majority of commercial creditors also discouraged the establishment of the SDRM. For example, the Institute for International Finance (IIF), a global association of financial institutions, was concerned that an international bankruptcy court could inhibit investor confidence, delay renewed access of debtor countries to capital markets that use the SDRM, and possibly lead to increased global financial instability through contagion effects in other emerging markets.[27] According to the IIF, the SDRM also might encourage moral hazard by encouraging other sovereign borrowers not to pay debts in order to receive stand-still protection.

The essential concern with the SDRM was whether the United States and the international community should condone an official stay on creditor rights through a litigation shield such as the SDRM. After two years of debate, the proposal was eventually bypassed at the spring 2003 IMF meetings, when the United States government threw its support behind including CACs in new bond contracts instead of creating a new IMF function.

However, only a few months after these meetings, the United Nations Security Council Iraq resolutions were passed, providing essentially the exact protections to Iraq that were rejected at the IMF. Financial analysts note that immunizing Iraq's debts from foreign claims through a U.N. Security Council

Resolution is a radical move in the history of sovereign debt negotiations. In the past, the U.S. government has taken a rather hands-off stance that let the financial markets resolve debt disputes. This approach, known as the "restrictive approach to state immunity," and codified through the Foreign Sovereign Immunities Act of 1976 (P.L. 94-583), established that foreign states are not immune from jurisdiction regarding, among other things, commercial activity including foreign debt.[28] Thus, the U.S. government typically allowed creditors to sue foreign governments regarding debt claims, and remained uninvolved in matters between U.S. creditors and foreign governments.[29]

The Iraq case thus illustrates that the United States and the international community are willing to shield a debtor from its creditors on an ad-hoc basis, case-by-case without a formal international bankruptcy regime. This can be accomplished multilaterally through U.N. Security Council Resolutions or bilaterally through executive orders. Since these measures were not taken in other recent financial crisis-afflicted countries, such as Argentina or Brazil, it appears that policymakers are only willing to use such measures selectively, and for countries that exhibit a perceived or potential threat to U.S. and international security. This understanding is made more explicit by implementing the stay on debt repayment through the United Nations, a political institution seen principally as focused on international security, rather than the International Monetary Fund, which is primarily a financial institution.

Flexibility of Paris Club Agreements

In addition to providing a precedent for a comprehensive debt shield, the Iraq case helped institutionalize increasing flexibility in Paris Club debt restructuring treatments. Prior to Iraq, Paris Club members adhered to a relatively strict set of rules to determine both which countries would be eligible for debt relief and the level of that debt relief, based on their economic situation. However, whenever a new situation arose where Paris Club members wanted to provide debt relief, but existing rules would not support it, new rules were created offering deeper and deeper debt reduction. Thus the Toronto Terms, introduced in 1988, begat Houston Terms in 1990, London Terms in 1991, Naples Terms in 1994, Lyon Terms in 1996, and finally Cologne Terms in 1999, each offering increased debt relief.

Cologne Terms, part of the Heavily Indebted Poor Country Program, allow for up to 100% debt cancellation for a select group of countries that the IMF and World Bank deem to be the most heavily indebted. The prevalence of debt reduction in Paris Club operations has led to what some have called the "slippery slope towards HIPCization," as increasing amounts of debt cancellation have been requested for countries on geo-political rather than economic grounds.[30] Pakistan, for example, is not a HIPC country, yet it is considered to be an integral partner in U.S. anti-terror efforts. When debt relief was sought for Pakistan in 2001, the Paris Club negotiated a special ad- hoc arrangement on near-Cologne terms even though Pakistan did not economically qualify to receive such treatment.

Instead of continuing to treat special cases, like Pakistan, under ad-hoc terms, the Paris Club formalized a new system of more flexible debt relief arrangements with Iraq under the new Evian Approach. As discussed earlier in the report, following Evian, potential debt-relief cases are divided into two groups, HIPC and non-HIPC. The 38 poor and indebted countries that are part of the HIPC program will continue to receive debt relief under the terms agreed to at Cologne. All other countries will be treated on a case-by-case basis with any debt relief determined by IMF debt sustainability analysis, with an option for three-part phased debt relief such as Iraq is receiving.

The introduction of Evian terms was crucial for Iraq's debt relief plan. "Without Evian in place," commented *Euromoney,* "it's hard to imagine the Paris Club members would have signed off on a deal as nakedly political as Iraq's."[31] Some argue that the Evian Approach is unfair, and opens the door even wider to political debt relief, using resources that could potentially go to increased debt relief or foreign assistance to poor and developing countries. For example, Indonesia, Kenya, and Georgia recently emerged from decades of authoritarian rule, and are saddled with extensive government debt, yet they received nowhere near the level of international exposure that has been given to Iraq.[32] "It's an outrageous double standard," according to Salih Booker, the head of Africa Action, a Washington-based lobbying group.[33]

It appears that the new flexibility evidenced by the introduction of the Evian approach is continuing. Following Evian, Paris Club members introduced even greater flexibility in 2005 by allowing countries to buy back their debt, a policy that had previously not been allowed. In 2004, Russia, using proceeds generated by record high petroleum prices, approached the Paris Club and requested to buyback some of its debt. Germany refused to participate, scuttling a Paris Club deal. A deal was eventually agreed on in May 2005 that allowed Russia to repay $15 billion in debts at par.[34] According to this agreement, Russia's debts were paid ahead of schedule without requiring a pre-payment penalty.

Following the Russia agreement, additional buyback deals were reached with Nigeria and Peru. In October 2005, a deal was reached where Nigeria was allowed to buy back some of its debt at a discount, leading to debt relief worth $18 billion and a total reduction of Nigeria's Paris Club debt from $36 billion to $6 billion. The Peru buyback, like Russia's, was at par, and will lead to Peru pre-paying $17 billion of its Paris Club debt.

As some analysts have illustrated, introducing flexibility into Paris Club arrangements was well underway prior to its handling of the Iraq case.[35] However, it appears that the precedent set by Iraq may open the door to increased debt relief for middle-income countries. Combined with the new willingness to engage in debt-buybacks, resolving international debt may be easier in the coming years.

Implementing an Odious Debt Strategy

Some analysts have argued that Iraq's debt is odious, and therefore may be repudiated under international law. There are three generally agreed upon components of the legal principle of odious debt: (1) the general population does not consent to the borrowing; (2) the proceeds do not benefit the general population or the state; (3) and the creditor knows both of these facts at the time of lending.[36] However, the concept of odious debt does not appear to be well established in international law and has never been cited by either a national or international tribunal as reason to repudiate a debt claim.[37]

Repudiating Iraq's debts under the concept of odious debts was raised by some Members of Congress in 2003 in H.R. 2482, *The Iraq Freedom From Debt Act*, introduced by Representative Carolyn Maloney. The bill, which was not enacted, called on the IMF and the World Bank to cancel Iraq's odious debt and called on Congress and the President to urge fellow Iraqi creditors to cancel their owed debt as well.

Iraqi officials have steadfastly claimed that they would not seek repudiation under the odious debt concept. In an interview with *Euromoney* in September 2004, Iraq's Minister of Finance, Adil Abdul Mahdi said:

> Iraq's need for very substantial debt relief derives from the economic realities facing a post- conflict country that has endured decades of financial corruption and mismanagement under the Saddam regime. Principles of

public international law such as the odious debt doctrine, whatever their legal vitality, are not the reason why Iraq is seeking this relief.[38]

Iraq preferred to seek a reduction of its debts through normal and official channels. The Paris Club's Iraq agreement, reached three months after the Minister's *Euromoney* interview, provided an 80% total reduction and set the parameters for the ongoing debt reduction efforts with non- Paris Club and commercial creditors. This allowed Iraq to receive its debt relief without the potential destruction of creditor relationships than can come about with a debt default.

In retrospect, it appears that an odious debt approach may have been difficult for Iraq since many of Iraq's debts were taken for economic development or commercial purposes and appear legitimate.[39] None of the debt in question was borrowed during the period when Iraq was under U.N. sanctions, when large amounts of Iraq's oil revenue were diverted for the construction of Saddam Hussein's palaces and other indulgences. It is also not evident that, at least to a degree greater than in other countries, the proceeds of the development loans were diverted for personal use or to fund oppression within Iraq.

Iraq's refusal to use an odious debt approach begs the question: under what circumstances could the odious debt principle be applied? In its current form, the odious debt doctrine, according to one analyst, "offers no meaningful guidance to shape decisions on lending to emerging markets."[40] One proposal is for the IMF or some other international body to assess a regime's legitimacy and make an odiousness determination, thus allowing any future government to declare any sovereign debt incurred by the previous "illegitimate" regime odious and repudiate it.[41] Such a sanctions regime may act as an incentive to creditors, both private and public, not to loan to problem regimes knowing that a successor government could legitimately repudiate the former regime's debts. U.S. foreign assistance to the new regime could also be made contingent on repudiation of odious debts.

On the other hand, the United States, or other nations, may not necessarily agree with the odiousness determination for various political reasons. It also may be difficult to make such a determination while a problem regime is in place, especially if other forms of political and economic statecraft are being employed.

However, given that the odious debt concept appears unusable in its current format, refashioning the odious debt concept as a sanctions regime represents one possible way to reduce the flow of financial resources to undesirable governments. Such a system would create additional incentives for creditor governments and the commercial sector to avoid lending to these regimes by creating the legal precedents necessary for a successor regime to repudiate so-called odious debt.

End Notes

[1] The Paris Club is the forum where major creditor countries negotiate terms for restructuring or resolving official government-to-government debt. It includes the United States and 18 other permanent members: Austria, Australia, Belgium, Canada, Denmark, Finland, France, Germany, Ireland, Italy, Japan, Netherlands, Norway, Russia, Spain, Sweden, Switzerland, and the United Kingdom. Other creditors are allowed to participate in negotiations on an ad-hoc basis.

[2] Creditor countries use different interest rates and levy different penalties for Iraq's payment arrears. Hence, the debt owed to each creditor can grow at different rates. In addition, Iraq could claim that it should not be expected to pay debt (or interest) accrued after the United Nations Security Council imposed sanctions in 1990 that made it illegal for financial institutions to process Iraq's financial transactions.

[3] Iraq's debts to the World Bank and the IMF were cleared in 2004, largely by contributions from Paris Club donor countries.

[4] Iraq Paris Club Debt Treatment, November 14, 2004. Available at http://www.clubdeparis.org/en/countries/countries.php?IDENTIFIANT=397&POSITION=0&PAY_ISO_ID=IQ&CONTINENT_ID=orient_afric_en&TYPE_T RT=&ANNEE=&INDICE_DET=.

[5] Iraq: First Review Under the Stand-By Arrangement and Financing Assurances Review Staff Report; International Monetary Fund, September 15, 2008. http://www.imf.org/external/pubs/ ft/scr/2008/cr08303.pdf

[6] For the full Jubilee Iraq compilation, see http://www.jubileeiraq.org/debt_today.htm.

[7] Meeting with Iraq's Commercial Claimants, *Iraq Debt Reconciliation Office*, May 4, 2005. http://www.eyidro.com

[8] Ibid.

[9] See CRS Report RL3 1944, *Iraq's Economy: Past, Present, Future*, by Jonathan E. Sanford.

[10] Statement of G7 Finance Ministers and Central Bank Governors, September 20, 2003.

[11] Many Paris Club policy decisions are decided during periodic finance ministers meetings of the G7 countries.

[12] More information on Paris Club debt treatment options is available at the Paris Club website: http://www.clubdeparis.org/.

[13] CRS Report RL33073, *Debt Relief for Heavily Indebted Poor Countries: Issues for Congress*, by Martin A. Weiss.

[14] Manmohan Singh and Jochen Andritzky, "How the Iraq Deal Was Done," *Euromoney*, September 2005.

[15] Iraq: First Review Under the Stand-By Arrangement and Financing Assurances Review Staff Report; International Monetary Fund, September 15, 2008. *http://www.imf.org/external/pubs/ft/scr/2008/cr08303.pdf*

[16] *Iraq Paris Club Comparability of Treatment Provision,* November 21, 2004. http://www.clubdeparis.org/en/ countries/ countries.php?CONTINENT_ID=orient_afric_en&DETAIL _DETTE_PAGE=4& IDENTIFIANT=397 &PAY_ISO_ID =IQ

[17] "Baker Secures Promises of Iraq Debt Relief from Gulf Oil States," *Agence France Presse*, January 21, 2004.

[18] See CRS Report RL3 1339, *Iraq: Post-Saddam Governance and Security*, by Kenneth Katzman.

[19] Iraq: First Review Under the Stand-By Arrangement and Financing Assurances Review Staff Report; International Monetary Fund, September 15, 2008. *http://www.imf.org/external/pubs/ft/scr/2008/cr08303.pdf*.

[20] The International Compact with Iraq: A Shared Vision, A Mutual Commitment, Draft Outline. Document is available at *http://www.iraqcompact.org/documents/ICI%20Outline%20Document%20-%20PG%20Version%20-* %205%20Sep.pdf. See also, *Final Report of the Iraq Study Group*, December 2006, p. 27. According to the study group, "Several U.S. and international officials told us that the compact could be an opportunity to seek greater international engagement in the country."

[21] Barry Schweid, "Saudi's Said Mulling Loan Relief for Iraq," *Associated Press*, April 18, 2007.

[22] The Iraq Debt Reconciliation Office. http://www.eyidro.com/

[23] Iraq Announces Conclusion of Commercial Debt Settlement. Available at http://www.eyidro.com/doc/Iraq_Annnounces_Conclusion_of_Commercial_Debt_Settlement.pdf

[24] Anna Gelpern, "What Iraq and Argentina Might Learn from Each Other," *Chicago Journal of International Law*, Summer 2005.

[25] "A New Approach to Sovereign Debt Restructuring: Preliminary Considerations, International Monetary Fund," November 30, 2001, available online at *http://www.imf.org/external/NP/pdr/sdrm/2001/113001.pdf*.

[26] Blustein, Paul, "IMF Cuts Disputed Clause from Debt Plan," *Washington Post*, January 8, 2003.

[27] Action Plan of the Institute for International Finance, Special Committee on Crisis Prevention and Resolution in Emerging Markets, April 2002.

[28] For more information on state immunity, see CRS Report RL31258, *Suits Against Terrorist States by Victims of Terrorism*, by Jennifer K. Elsea; and Tom McNamara, *A Primer on Foreign Sovereign Immunity*, Davis Graham & Stubbs LLP, available at http://www.worldservicesgroup.com/publications.asp?action=article&artid=1223.

[29] Gelpern, p. 396.

[30] Callaghy, Thomas M. "The Paris Club and International Economic Governance: Double Crisis and Debt," in Brigitte Granville and Vinod Aggarwal ed., *Sovereign Debt: Origins, Management and Restructuring*, Royal Institute for International Affairs, 2003, p. 165.

[31] Manmohan Singh and Jochen Andritzky, "Paris Club Members Adapt to New Rules,"*Euromoney*, September, 2005.

[32] Joseph Siegle, "After Iraq, let's forgive some other debts," *International Herald Tribune*, February 19, 2004.

[33] Quoted in Sudarson Raghavan, "African Advocates to U.S.: Reduce Our Debt Like Iraq's," *The Miami Herald*, February 20, 2004.

[34] "Paris Club Reaches $15B In Debt Repayment Deal With Russia," *MosNews*, May 13, 2005, available at http://www.mosnews.com/money/2005/05/13/parisclubfinal.shtml.

[35] See Lex Rieffel, *Restructuring Sovereign Debt: The Case for Ad Hoc Machinery*, Brookings Institution Press, 2003.

[36] Todd Moss, Scott Standley, and Nancy Birdsall, "Double Standards, Debt Treatment, and World Bank Country Classification: The Case of Nigeria," *Center for Global Development*, November 2004, p. 33, and Gelpern, p. 403.

[37] Gelpern, pg. 406. See also the discussion in CRS Report RL3 1944, *Iraq's Economy: Past, Present, Future*, by Jonathan E. Sanford.

[38] Cited in Gelpern, p. 406.

[39] CRS Report RL3 1944, *Iraq's Economy: Past, Present, Future*, by Jonathan E. Sanford.

[40] Gelpern, 412.

[41] Michael Kremer and Seema Jayachandran, "Odious Debt: When Dictators Borrow, Who Repays the Loan?" *The Brookings Review*, Spring 2003.

Chapter Sources

The following chapters have been previously published:

Chapter 1 – This is an edited, excerpted and augmented edition of a United States Congressional Research Service publication, Report Order Code R41122, dated March 11, 2010.

Chapter 2 – This is an edited, excerpted and augmented edition of a United States Congressional Research Service publication, Report Order Code R41239, dated June 4, 2010.

Chapter 3 – This is an edited, excerpted and augmented edition of a United States Congressional Research Service publication, Report Order Code R41167, dated May 14, 2010.

Chapter 4 – This is an edited, excerpted and augmented edition of a United States Congressional Research Service publication, Report Order Code R41029, dated April 28, 2010.

Chapter 5 – This is an edited, excerpted and augmented edition of a United States Congressional Research Service publication, Report Order Code RL31590, dated February 3, 2010.

Chapter 6 – This is an edited, excerpted and augmented edition of a United States Congressional Research Service publication, Report Order Code RL33376, dated January 26, 2009.

INDEX

F

G

H

I

T

U

V

W

Y

Z